REPRESENTATIVE MEN

OF

SOUTHERN INDIA

REPRESENTATIVE MEN

OF

SOUTHERN INDIA

PARAMASWARAN PILLAI G.

GYAN

Published by

GYAN

Gyan Publishing House
5, Ansari Road
Daryaganj, New Delhi-110002
Phone: 011-47034999, 9811692060
E-mail: books@gyanbooks.com

Distribution Network
gyanbooks.com
India, USA, Canada, UK, Australia, France

ISBN : 978-81-212-9444-7 (PB)
First Published, 1896

2nd Impression 2023

Printed at: Gyan Press, Delhi.

REPRESENTATIVE MEN OF SOUTHERN INDIA
Author: PARAMASWARAN PILLAI G.

REPRESENTATIVE MEN

OF

SOUTHERN INDIA.

REPRESENTATIVE MEN

OF

SOUTHERN INDIA.

Madras:

AT THE PRICE CURRENT PRESS.

1896.

PREFACE.

It is singular that while the biographies of several eminent men of Bengal and Bombay have been published, India knows little or nothing of the greatest men of Southern India. Madras has given birth to several distinguished men who cannot suffer in comparison with the best men of other parts of India. Yet, no attempt has hitherto been made to publish a permanent record of their lives for the information of the people of India as a whole and for the instruction and edification of the rising generation of Southern India in particular. About two years ago, it struck me that I may make an attempt however humble, in this direction, and accordingly opened the columns of the *Madras Standard* for the publication of the biographical sketches of eminent Indians. Out of the numerous sketches that have since appeared under the heading "Our Portrait Gallery," I have selected for separate publication the lives of twelve representative men who are held in high esteem by the people of this Presidency, both European and Indian. Among the Princes and Zemindars of Southern India, none are better known than Sir Rama Varma, the late Maharajah of Travancore and Sir Vizia Rama, the late Maharajah of Vizianagram. Sir Madava Row, V. Ramiengar, C. V. Runga Charlu and A. Seshia Sastri are acknowledged on all hands to be the most distinguished of South Indian Statesmen. As a Linguist, C. V. Runganada Sastri has left behind him a reputation which is unique. As a Jurist none has surpassed Sir T. Muthusawmy Aiyar. In the field of education, nobody has yet been found to take the place of Rai Bahadur Gopal Row and Rai Bahadur Runganada Mudaliar. And there breathed not sturdier patriots than Gazulu Lakshminarasu Chetty and Salem Ramasawmy Mudaliar. All these men—with one exception—are men of the past. It has been with the greatest difficulty that the particulars of their lives have been obtained. I need scarcely add that it would have been impossible for me to publish this book, even in its present imperfect form without the willing co-operation of some of their relatives, friends and admirers. Some of them have contributed the sketches as they originally appeared in the *Madras Standard*, others have supplied me with materials to work upon: others again have given me information by word of mouth or in writing scarcely less important than the information obtained in other ways. To all these men I wish to take this opportunity of expressing my deep obligation; and among them none have greater claims on my gratitude than Rai Bahadur V. Kishnama Chariar, Professor P. Sundram Pillai, M. A., Professor S. Sathianadhan, M. A., LL. B., R. Ragagopala Chariar, B.A., B.L., C. V. Visvanatha Sastri, B.A., B.L., S. Sitarama Sastri, B.A., T. Lakshmana Row, B.A., O. Kandasawmy Chetty and M. P. Duraisamy Iyer. I have also utilised the information contained in a few books and pamphlets and among them must be mentioned, Hansards' Parliamentary Debates, Administration Reports of Baroda, Travancore and Pudukota, Reprint of an article on "A native Statesman" from the *Calcutta Review* and of another article on "Sir Madava Row," from the Journal of the Poona Sarvajanik Sahba, and a life of Rai Bahadur T. Gopal Row, by Mr. Narasimmiah, B. A., B. L. None of the sketches appear in this book in the form in which they were published in the *Madras Standard*. All of them have been revised, some have been almost entirely re-written, while one or two have undergone comparatively little change. It has not been possible to preserve any order in the publication of the lives: were it not that materials for two or three of these were obtained but very recently, the lives of Runga Charlu and Seshia Sastri would have followed those of Sir Madava Row and V. Ramiengar. The book is not free from such and similar defects and my only justification for its publication is the absence of any better book containing the biographies of the eminent men of Southern India; and this attempt to sketch the details of their lives has been made in the hope that it may tempt those who are better fitted to do the work to complete the perfect figure of those men.

G. P.

MADRAS,
4th May 1896.

CONTENTS.

INTRODUCTION.

"The names and memories of great men are a dowry of a nation." It may be questioned whether the men, the story of whose lives is told in the following pages, may be reckoned great. Not certainly in the sense in which the heroes of the world are great. But there is a relative greatness as well as an absolute greatness. Emerson counts him a great man "who inhabits a higher sphere of thought into which other men rise with labour and difficulty; he has but to open his eyes to see things in a true light and in large relations, whilst they must make painful corrections and keep a vigilant eye on many sources of error." Beaconsfield defines a great man as "one who affects the mind of his generation." In either of these senses, the men whose lives are embodied in this volume may be considered great. But whether great or not, they are the best products of that happy welding of the keen intellect of the East with the sturdy self-reliance and energy of the

West. All of them are men of the nineteenth century "who have imbibed what is best of the wisdom that Europe can teach without breaking away from all their old moorings." The earliest of them was born in 1806 and one of them still lives—"a prosperous gentleman." Their lives, therefore, well-nigh cover the century.

G. Lakshminarasu Chetty was born in the first decade of the present century and it was not till twenty years after his birth that the First "Committee of Public Instruction" was appointed in Madras. His school education was, therefore, not worth the name. Runganada Sastri was born towards the close of the second decade: Sir Madava Row, Ramiengar and Seshia Sastri during the third decade: and Runga Charlu and Sir Muthusawmy Aiyar in the beginning of the fourth decade: and these, therefore, had the advantage of being educated in the High School of the Madras University which was established in 1840. Gopal Row was born in the fourth decade, Runganada Mudaliar in the fifth and Ramasawmy Mudaliar in the sixth: and all these, the two latter particularly, had a University education, the Madras University having been established in 1857. The remaining two, Sir Vizia Rama who was born in the third decade and Sir Rama Varma who was born in the fourth, having been princes of the blood royal were educated privately.

Before the birth of any of these, the British power had been firmly established in Southern

India. The last local effort to defy the British power was the Vellore Mutiny which took place in the very year in which the earliest of our heroes was born. There were several wars and disturbances in other parts of India subsequent to that date, but Southern India was scarcely affected by them. Looking back, we find that in 1858, the year of the consolidation of British Power in India, all our heroes had a contemporaneous existence. Lakshminarasu Chetty was then in the plenitude of his power, engaged in demanding a pledge of religious neutrality from the British authorities, encouraged by his previous successes in the political field of battle: Runganada Sastri to the evident surprise and delight of judges of the High Court, was displaying his mastery over fourteen different languages as Chief Interpreter: Sir Vizia Rama was in charge of his Zemindary devising means and methods of enriching his estate and winning the esteem and approbation of the British authorities: Sir Rama Varma was addressing stirring letters to the *Indian Statesman* on Travancore topics: Sir Madava Row had just then been entrusted with the reins of administration in Travancore: Ramiengar was working hard as a Deputy Collector in Tanjore: Runga Charlu was acquiring revenue experience as Tahsildar of Saidapet: Seshia Sastri was employed in improving the administration of Masulipatam as Head Sheristadar: Sir Muthusamy Aiyer was winning laurels as a District Munsif: Gopal Row was distinguishing himself as First Assistant in the Provincial School at Kumbakonam:

Runganada Mudaliar was a mere boy who was being carefully educated at home by his father: and Salem Ramasawmy Mudelliar was being rocked in the cradle by his mother—all consciously, we suppose, in the cradle of future distinction.

Sir Rama Varma and Sir Vizia Rama were the best specimens of Native Princes in Southern India. The one was the ruler of the most important Native State in the Madras Presidency; and the other was in charge of the biggest Zemindary. Both were highly cultured; both were of polished manners; and both administered their dominions with marked ability. Their merits are particularly worthy of appreciation, as in this country as well as elsewhere,

> "Seldom, alas! the power of logic reigns
> With much sufficiency in royal brains."

Sir Grant Duff spoke of Sir Rama Varma as "a typical example of the influence of English thought upon the South Indian mind." Sir Rama Varma was a man of such uncommon parts that he would have made his mark in any profession, if he was not born in the purple. As a statesman, he would have been a formidable rival to Sir Madava Row, Ramiengar, Runga Charlu and Seshia Sastri. If he had followed the profession of the schoolmaster, he would have become as great an educationist as Gopal Row or Runganada Mudaliar. He was the best specimen of an educated Indian prince. What Sir Rama Varma was among rulers of native States in India, that Sir Vizia Rama was among Zemindars. Sir Vizia Rama ought to serve as a model to the young Zemindars of these days some of whom, though well educated, have become incapable of administering the affairs of their Zemindaris. Sir Vizia Rama was in charge of his Zemindari for thirty years and when he died, he died full of years and honors, leaving a handsome surplus of fifteen lakhs of Rupees to his son and successor, in spite of his numerous private charities and public benefactions.

Sir Madava Row, Ramiengar, Runga Charlu and Seshia Sastri represent the highest types of native statesmanship in India. They were the pupils of that exemplary schoolmaster, Eyre Burton Powell and all of them were Proficients of the old High School. One of them, Sir Madava Row was Dewan of three native States, Travancore Indore and Baroda; another, Seshia Sastri was Dewan of two native States, Travancore and Pudukota ; and the remaining two, Runga Charlu and Ramiengar were Dewans of Mysore and Travancore, respectively. Three of them, Sir Madava Row, Ramiengar and Seshia Sastri were Dewans of the same State, Travancore. The services of Sir Madava Row were confined almost wholly to native States; and he established the ground work of his reputation in Travancore. Runga Charlu won his spurs partly in British territory and partly in Mysore. But both Ramiengar and Seshia Sastri established their reputation in the service of the Madras Government, which they enhanced by their work in native States. Sir Madava Row did equally good work in Travancore and Baroda. In Indore, he did little or nothing. The chief scene of Seshia Sastri's labours was Pudukota where he ruled for sixteen years though he was first called to Travancore. Ramiengar's attention was absorbed in Travancore as Runga Charlu's was in Mysore. But, unlike Sir Madava Row, Ramiengar and Seshia Sastri, Runga Charlu was cut away in the very midst of his labours. Sir Madava Row spent several years in Madras after his retirement from Baroda. Seshia Sastri lives in honourable retirement after completing his labours in Pudukota. Ramiengar left Travancore only after seven years of hard toil. But Runga Charlu had barely two years during which he had to establish his reputation. Ramiengar and Runga Charlu were only Dewans or Prime Ministers. But Sir Madava Row and Seshia Sastri had the rare fortune of becoming Dewan-Regents or Dewans invested with royal powers.

Circumstances make the man and though the man is not the less esteemed on that account, it is worthy of note that special circumstances favoured almost all these statesmen. Travancore had attained the worst stage of misrule when Sir Madava Row was made Dewan. Pudukotta was no whit better, when Seshia Sastri was called upon to take up the reins of administration. Runga Charlu had free scope in moulding the administration of Mysore after his own mind. And Ramiengar had the peculiar fortune of serving a Maharajah who was competent to be his own Dewan. All of them had to surmount difficulties arising from their being alien to the people whose affairs they were called upon to administer. Sir Madava Row was viewed as a 'foreigner' more in Baroda than even in Travancore. Ramiengar was looked upon as a stranger all the time he was in Travancore. Runga Charlu was subjected to grave accusations in Mysore as he had the misfortune to be a Madrasi. And Seshia Sastri had his own share of unpopularity in Pudukotta. These statesmen have left an indelible mark of their individuality on the administrations of Baroda, Mysore, Travancore and Pudukota. "Constitute Government how you please," says Burke "infinitely the greater part of it must depend upon the exercise of powers which are left at large to the prudence and uprightness of Ministers of State. Even all the use and potency of laws depends upon them." The modern history of these native States bears undoubted testimony to the prudence and uprightness of the four Ministers.

Runganada Sastri and Sir Muthusawmy Aiyar were both Judges. The one was the first native Judge of the Court of Small Causes and the other the first native Judge of the High Court. But Runganada Sastri was better known as a linguist than as a jurist. He was the first Proficient of the old High School. It is surprising how he could have mastered fourteen different languages, in many of which he became proficient. His scholarship was the object of admiration among his European contemporaries. Since his days, Southern India has not produced a single man who as a linguist could be spoken of in the same breath with him and considering the tendencies of modern education, it is doubtful whether any will take his place hereafter. Sir Muthusawmy Aiyar was a great jurist. He has raised the reputation of Indians for judicial work and his talent was of no mean order.

In these days when the schoolmaster armed with his primer is trusted against the soldier in full military array, the services of Gopal Row and Runganada Mudaliar cannot fail to be estimated at their true worth. Both of them were for some years employed as Professors in the Presidency College. Mathematics was the forte of both but Gopal Row excelled in the teaching of English as well and Runganada Mudaliar of philosophy. Speaking of Turgot, Mr. John Morley says "It is hardly to be denied that mathematical genius and philosophic genius do not always go together. The precision, definiteness and accurate limitations of the method of the one are usually unfriendly to the brooding, tentative, uncircumscribed meditation which is the productive humour in the other." Runganada Mudalliar was an exception. In fact, his special claims to be remembered by posterity are based on the fact that he was a man of wide and varied culture. His English was as good as his Mathematics and his Philosophy. Gopal Row and Runganada Mudaliar possessed that magnetic charm which creates a mysterious sympathy between the teacher and the taught. Both of them excelled in powers of conversation and to this probably may be traced, at least partially the great influence they possessed over society.

Lakshminarasu Chetty and Ramasawmy Mudaliar are the best types of two classes of patriots, the old and the new. But patriotism is no profession. By profession, the one was a merchant and the other a lawyer. Lakshminarasu Chetty lived in days when he had not merely to educate himself but educate the people. It required no small amount of pluck, moral courage and ability to carry on political agitation in the days of Lakshminarasu Chetty and that he should have carried it on for years together and so successfully till the Madras Government forgetting the odium in which he was once held, honored him by soliciting his assistance in the administration of the presidency reflects no little credit on Lakshminarasu Chetty and on the Madras Government itself. Lakshminarasu Chetty's patriotism was not lip deep. He not merely agitated for the redress of the people's grievances but plunged his hands deep into his purse for the purpose. Ramasawmy Mudaliar was an ardent Congressman. Both Lakshminarasu Chetty and Ramasawmy Mudaliar had great faith in political associations as auxiliary to political agitation. The former started the "Madras Native Association" and became its President. The latter assisted at the birth of the "Mahajana Sabha" and became its

Vice-President. The lives of both showed that humility or modesty was not inconsistent with advanced views in politics.

Gopal Row and Sir Muthusawmy Aiyar were known for their great perseverance. The one passed the B. A. Examination and the other the B. L,, very creditably in the first class long after they had both ceased to be students and while taxed with heavy professional work. Both had "borne their faculties" very meek. Sir Madava Row and Gopal Row dabbled in Maratha poetry. The poems composed by the former were simple and those of the latter were appreciated for their chasteness of style. Runganada Mudaliar and Ramasawmy Mudaliar were the recognised leaders of Hindu Society during the latter part of their career. Runganada Mudaliar in private society was always a powerfnl centre of attraction. His speech, his manners, and his general behaviour produced such a charming impression on the mind of the public that he was one of their greatest favourites. Of Ramasawmy Mudaliar, it may be truly said that "there seemed a pool of honey about his heart which lubricated all his speech and action with fine jets of mead." Runganada Mudaliar and Ramasawmy Mudaliar were two of the most charming of men. If one was like the flower which by unfolding its petals sheds light and fragrance around, the other was like the bud whose very form is a picture of modesty concealing beauty and sweetness within. Southern India has known no better conversationalists than Seshia Sastri, Gopal Row and Runganada Mudaliar. In conversation, Gopal Row was impressive: Runganada Mudaliar brilliant; and Seshia Sastri's conversational powers are marked by an ease, vividness, and humour rarely to be met with.

The subjects of our sketches were not merely contemporary men; most of them knew each other intimately and had much in common. Runganada Sastri, Sir Madava Row, Seshia Sastri, Runga Charlu, Sir Muthusawmy Aiyar and Ramiengar were Proficients of the old High School, all except the last named having been placed in the First Class. Sir Muthusawmy Iyer was both a Proficient and a graduate of the Madras University. Gopal Row, Runganada Mudaliar and Ramasawmy Mudaliar were graduates. Lakshminarasu Chetty, Runganada Sastri, Ramiengar and Seshia Sastri were members of the Madras Legislative Council. Sir Vizia Rama was a member of the Imperial Legislative Council. Sir Rama Varma, Sir Madava Row and Seshia Sastri were offered seats in the Imperial Legislative Council. Runganada Mudaliar competed for a seat in the local Legislative Council as the representative of the University and polled equal votes with his rival candidate. Runganada Sastri was nominated a Fellow of the Madras University in 1857: Sir Rama Varma in 1861: Sir Madava Row in 1862: Gopal Row in 1867: Runga Charlu and Ramiengar in 1868: Sir Muthusawmy Aiyer and Runganada Mudaliar in 1872: and

Ramasawmy Mudaliar in 1887. Sir Madava Row, Ramiengar, Runganada Sastri and Sir Muthusawmy Aiyar were invited to attend the Imperial Assemblage in 1877 and were offered the Delhi medal. Sir Madava Row and Ramiengar were invited to give evidence before the Parliamentary Finance Commission in England. Sir Rama Varma was a Knight Grand Commander of the Order of the Star of India : Sir Vizia Rama and Sir Madava Row were Knight Commanders: Ramiengar, Seshia Sastri and Lakshminarasu Chetty were Companions. Sir Muthusawmi Aiyar was a Knight Commander of the Order of the Indian Empire : Runga Charlu was a Companion. Gopal Row, Runganada Mudaliar and Ramasawmy Mudaliar were Rai Bahadurs. Sir Madava Row was a member of the Malabar Land Tenure commission : Sir Muthusawmy Aiyer of the Malabar Marriage Commission: Runganada Mudaliar of the Education Commission: and Ramasawmy Mudaliar of the Public Service Commission. Sir Madava Row, Sir Muthusawmy Aiyar and Runganada Mudaliar had the honor of being called upon by the Governor to deliver Convocation addresses to graduates. Ramiengar, Ramasawmy Mudaliar and Runganada Mudaliar were Municipal Commissioners of the City of Madras and Ramiengar Runganada Sastri, Lakshminarasu Chetty and Ramasawmy Mudaliar were Trustees of Pachaiappa's Charities.

It is interesting to trace the close connection that existed between these eminent men. Runganada Sastri was Sir Madava Row's tutor for a short time: Sir Rama Varma was Sir Madava Row's pupil: Ramiengar was Sir Rama Varma's Minister: Runga Charlu was taken into the Mysore service at the instance of Sir Rama Varma: and Seshia Sastri was Dewan of Travancore when Sir Rama Varma was heir apparent to the throne. Sir Madava Row was Sir Muthusawmy Aiyar's Patron: Runganada Mudaliar won the prizes instituted in Pachaiappa's College by Sir Rama Varma and Sir Madava Row: Ramasawmy Mudaliar was Runganada Mudaliar's pupil in the Presidency College. and Gopal Row accompanied his father to Travancore on the invitation of Sir MadavaRow's father. On Lakshminarasu Chetty's death, among those that contributed to his memorial, the most prominent were Sir Rama Varma and Sir Madava Row.

It is also interesting to know what these eminent men thought of each other. In the opinion of Sir Rama Varma, Sir Madava Row had done for Travancore "what Pericles did for Athens" and "what Crowwell did for England." Sir Madava Row thought Seshia Sastri was "one of the most distinguished natives India had produced" and "intrinsically a very good man." Seshia Sastri considered Ramasawmy Mudaliar "one of the best young men of whom the University may be proud." Muthusawmy Aiyar was inspired "with a feeling of high esteem and regard for Runganada Mudaliar." Of Sir Muthusawmy Aiyar, Runganada Mudaliar said "he is out and out the best man that modern

India has produced so far as intellectual acumen is concerned." Sir Muthusawmy Aiyar thought Runga Charlu "was really a great man possessing a colossal intellect while his powers of organisation were very astonishing." Of Gopal Row, he said, "he is the only person whom I have throughout in life admired." And Runganada Mudaliar admitted that he felt the death of Gopal Row "as a loss to the native community of Southern India."

Almost all our heroes were intellectual men and each of them had his own favourite author of whom he made a special study. Thus we find that the favourite book of Sir Madava Row was Gibbon: of Sir Muthusawmy Aiyar, Goldsmith: of Seshia Sastri, Addison: of Sir Rama Varma, Macaulay, of Gopal Row, Shelley: of Runganada Mudaliar, Shakespeare: and of Runganada Sastri, Cicero.

It is worthy of note that at least five of these eminent men were men "whose life in low estate began" and who broke their "birth's invidious bar" and made "by force their merit known." Sir Muthusawmy Aiyar began life on a salary of Re. 1 per mensem. Ramiengar's father was hardly able to educate his son. It would have been impossible for Runga Charlu to get himself educated without the generous help he received from some of his distant relatives. Runganada Sastri owed his education entirely to the generosity of a District Judge. Seshia Sastri was equally poor. All these were men whom poverty had inured to hardship and necessity had compelled to exertion; and the habits they had acquired in the early school of difficulty had served them in good stead in later years.

None of the deceased eminent men has been blessed with long life. Sir Madava Row and Sir Muthusawmy Aiyar died in their sixty-third year: Lakshminarasu Chetty and Runganada Sastri attained the age of sixty-two: Ramiengar was sixty-one years old at the time of his death: Gopal Row was fifty-four: Sir Vizia Rama was fifty-three: Runga Charlu was fifty-two: Sir Rama Varma forty-eight: Runganada Mudaliar forty-six: and Ramasawmy Mudaliar forty. None of them, it will be seen, attained the age of seventy: only five attained the age of sixty: while three did not attain even the age of fifty.

The lives of the Proficients of the old High School tempt us to make a few observations. Though their studies did not embrace all the higher branches of learning now included in the curriculum for the B. A. or M. A. degree, the old Proficients were as men of culture, much superior to the modern Bachelors of Arts and Masters of Arts. This may be due to the fact that in these days when hundreds of students are compelled to read together in the same class, the teacher is not in a position to devote that attention to each student individually which he would have been able to devote if his pupils were few in number. But apart from this, we think the result is due to a large extent to the fact that the Professors and masters of those days took a deep interest in the welfare of their students and attended more to their general culture than to their ability to pass examinations. Speaking of that veteran educationist, Mr. Powell, Runga Charlu said, "when I recall to my mind the singleness of purpose and devotion with which he gave himself up to the education of those placed under his care during a period attended with many discouragements and difficulties, the many hours, both in and out of school time, which he devoted to his pupils, the many afternoons even during holidays which he gladly spent with his pupils in reading some English authors not embraced in the school course or in showing them chemical and other scientific experiments in his private laboratory and the nights which he sat up to show them the wonders of the planetary world with expensive telescopes provided out of his own moderate means and when I reflect that he was able to continue with undiminished interest these by no means easy labours during the period of nearly quarter of a century, it is impossible not to be overpowered with a feeling of admiration and gratitude ? Remarkable as he was for the thoroughness and precision of his teaching and the extensive range of information which he was able to place before his students, that which most impressed their mind was, I think, the silent but enduring influence of his high and exemplary character." Teachers like Powell and Porter are extremely rare in these days and rarer indeed are those who labour to make their students real men of culture rather than render them fit merely to receive the hall mark of the University.

Another feature which cannot escape observation is the cordiality of feeling which existed between Europeans and Indians in the early days of English education in India and the deep and abiding and even paternal interest some Anglo-Indians took in the well-being and prosperity of intelligent Indians. This may be partially explained by the fact that the number of educated natives in those days was few. Nevertheless, we find it difficult to resist the conclusion that these European gentlemen, apart from the nobility and magnanimity of their character were more deeply attached to the land of their adoption. Among those who had worked in the interests of the natives in Southern India, none were better known than John Bruce Norton and William Holloway. John Bruce Norton closely watched the career of almost every one of our eminent men. Lakshminarasu Chetty was his great personal friend, and it was mainly through his exertions that a memorial was raised in that patriot's honor after his death. Sir Rama Varma was a frequent contributor to the newspapers edited by Norton and they kept up a correspondence which ceased only with the death of one of them. Of Sir Madava Row, Norton spoke in the highest terms year after year at the anniversary of Pachaiappa's College. Ramiengar became a Trustee of Pachaiappa's charities at the instance of Norton. Runganada Sastri was held in high esteem by Norton and he gave public expression to his scholarship more than once in Pachaiappa's College. Norton was one of those who early appreciated the merits of Sir Muthusawmy Aiyar and deplored the waste of "much judicial talent" in the Revenue Department. He also bore testimony to the high character of Seshia Sastri. In Runganada Mudaliar, he espied "a young man of singular promise." Holloway was another warm friend of the people of India. It was under Holloway's training that Sir Muthusawmy Aiyar developed his faculty for analysing judgments. He was one of the earliest to appreciate the worth of Gopal Row. The Prize essay of Runganada Mudaliar in Pachaiappa's College was examined by Holloway and it was on the recommendation of Holloway that Ramasawmy Mudaliar was trained as an apprentice under the then Advocate-General. Holloway took delight in reading the official reports of Seshia Sastri. Runganada Sastri owed his education, his culture, in fact, everything of which he was proud to the noble and generous help and the unexampled liberality of a District Judge, Casamajor. To Ramiengar, Runga Charlu and Seshia Sastri, George Noble Taylor was a common patron.

The lives of some of the eminent men of Southern India bear testimony to the fact that the British Government in spite of their just laws and love of fair play afford little scope for distinction to natives and give them little encouragement. We wonder what would have been the fate of Sir Madava Row, Runga Charlu, Ramiengar and Seshia Sastri if there were no Native States in India. Ramiengar would have retired as Superintendent of Stamps or Inspector-General of Registration; to Seshia Sastri no more responsible place would have been open than that of Head Sheristadar of the Board of Revenue; the ambition of Runga Charlu would have leapt no higher than the appointment of a Deputy Collector: and Sir Madava Row would have at best been an efficient revenue officer. These offices would have afforded little room for the display of their intellectnal attainments or for the exercise of their statesmanlike instincts and they would have lived and died like any other plodding, perspiring official in the Revenue Department under Government. They might have perished unseen, wasting their sweetness in the desert air; and posterity would have known little or nothing of them.

Even Gopal Row and Runganada Mudaliar whose abilities were of the highest, were the lesser lights they were on account of the restrictions placed on them by the British Government. In spite of his great reputation as a teacher, his recognised abitity and the success and distinction with which he had conducted the duties of Principal for three years in the Kumbakonam College, Gopal Row was never confirmed as Principal and it was several years subsequently that he was admitted even into the graded service as Professor of History and Political Economy in the Presidency College. Runganada Mudaliar was not treated a whit better. A man of his genius had to act as Professor for sixteen years in some capacity or other before he was confirmed as Professor of Mathematics in the Presidency College ! Even Sir. T. Muthusawmy Aiyar could only *act* as Chief Justice. He was permitted to soar no higher.

Another fact which we deplore is that these men though they were the best types of educated men in Southern India have left behind them nothing of permanent literary interest to the rising generation. Sir Rama Varma has written but a few essays on educational and other topics. Sir Madava Row is responsible only for "Hints on the training of native children." Such a linguist as Runganada Sastri is not known as the author of any book. No treatise on law marks the memory of Sir T. Muthusawmy Aiyar. The claims of Gopal Row and Runganada Mudaliar to immortality are based on the metrical translation of "Goldsmith's Hermit" in Marathi and "Kachikalandakam" in Tamil, respectively. Few men possess the requisite ability to write books. But it cannot be denied that at least some of these men could have left some work more enduring behind them if they had made an effort. It strikes us that Indians generally however highly cultured, are wanting in system and method in their work and do not utilise their leisure hours in the proper manner. It was the ambition of more than one of these men to labour in the production of some substantial work; and though they did not lack capacity, they postponed the performance to the very last till they were either cut away in the vigour of their manhood or found it too late to make the attempt.

In the following pages, there is abundant testimony to show that many of the eminent men of Southern India were convinced of the necessity of removing some of the social evils rampant in Hindu society. Sir Madava Row advocated female education and was opposed to early marriage. Runganada Sastri was a great believer in female education. He was the first to point out the evils of Hindu customs and to attribute the backward condition of the Hindus to those evils. Sir Muthusawmy Aiyer thought there was no foundation for the belief that a marriage contracted after maturity was illegal and held that re-marriage was as necessary in the case of young widows whose marriage had been consummated as in the case of virgin widows. Gopal Row considered early marriage the bane and curse of Hindu society. Enforced widowhood, he thought, was unquestionably productive of much misery. Runganada Mudaliar advocated social reform but insisted upon social reformers carrying the masses with them. Lakshminarasu Chetty had great faith in the education of women and encouraged the marriage of widows. There were others also who sympathised with social reform in the same spirit. But how few among them have given a practical turn to their sympathies by boldly putting themselves forward as examples to other members of their community! If they had done so, considering the very great influence they exercised over the people, the result would have been something of abiding interest to the whole native community.

Here we must bid adieu to our heroes in the hope that however imperfect our performance, the lives of a dozen of the best men to whom Southern India has given birth cannot but be of permanent interest to the rising generation. "Such men are," as Emerson says "the collyrium to clear our eyes from egotism and enable us to see other people and their works".

G. PARAMASWARAN PILLAI.

MADRAS
4th May, 1896.

SIR RAMA VARMA, G.C.S.I.,

LATE MAHARAJAH OF TRAVANCORE.

Sir Rama Varma, late Maharajah of Travancore, was born on the 19th May 1837. His father, a member of the family of "Koil Tampurans" of Tiruvallah in Travancore was a nobleman of spotless character who in addition to his great natural intelligence, possessed ripe scholarship in Sanscrit and a tolerably fair knowledge of English. His mother Rukmini Bai also possessed sufficient scholarship in Sanscrit to compose easy and sensible verses in that difficult tongue. Prince Rama Varma was the last of a family of seven children of whom three died early and two were declared imbeciles. One of the three deceased died just six days before Prince Rama Varma's birth, which event naturally gave a severe shock to the mother and probably affected also the constitution of the child she was then about to deliver. At the end of the eighth week after his birth his mother died, which again must have further enfeebled the child's delicate physique. The early training of the boy, therefore, fell to the lot of his grand aunt, Rani Parvati Bai, and his own father. Of both, His Highness retained to the last the kindliest of recollection. His reverence for his father was almost unbounded and he always thought of him as the very model of self-control and rigid, unbending honesty. It was the father who mainly directed the early education of the Prince. As usual he began in his fifth year his Malayalam and Sanscrit studies. Unlike most of those who now seek instruction in our English Schools, he first obtained a sound and thorough training in his own vernacular, supplemented by a knowledge of that Indian classic so essential to Malayalam. In his ninth year he was taught the English alphabet by a retired Dewan, Subba Row, who, having been the English tutor to his uncles is still spoken of in Travancore as "English" Subba Row. The early studies of the Prince were often interrupted by bodily ailments. Nevertheless, whenever he did attend to his work, he did so most zealously. Perfunctory performance of any function seems to have been wholly foreign to his nature, and the strict discipline of his father rendered it further impossible. Thus was an indomitable will slowly nurtured in him which while submissive to all rightful authority, sternly defied any power encroaching upon his own rights. In 1849 he was taken seriously ill with the first signs of consumption which, while weakening his body, seems to have only strengthened his will.

It was while Prince Rama Varma was thus getting his character formed and struggling to pick up what elements of knowledge his own tutors in the land could provide, that the new educational policy of the British Indian Government produced a man who could guide the eager young mind into the higher walks of learning. Five years after the birth of the Prince, was instituted in Madras a High school for the secular education of the Indians,—the first mark of the new era of Higher Education in the Madras Presidency. One of the earliest eminent products of this High School was T. Madhava Row, who soon after obtaining his Proficiency Degree, was deemed cultured enough to officiate for his master, Mr. Powell, as Professor in that very institution. By the time Madhava Row had completed his education in Madras, Prince Rama Varma of Travancore was prepared to commence his own under him. Having been asked to select a competent tutor, the choice of the Madras Government naturally fell on Madhava Rao, who besides being one of the foremost scholars of the day, had special claims upon Travancore as the son of one and nephew of another Dewan. In August 1849 Madhava Rao was appointed tutor. The tuition continued for nearly four years, and while it cannot be said to have partaken of the character of a strict scholastic education, the course was nevertheless broad and sound. It embraced general literature and the elements of the experimental sciences, and was specially suited to set in motion a naturally studious mind in the direction of varied and useful activity. In this tuition, the Prince's father co-operated heartily, and his influence ever tended to confirm and expand the character he had already impressed upon his son in his infancy. In July 1853, Madhava Rao took up an appointment in the general administration of the State, and with it the period of the Prince's tuition may be said to have come to an end. But unlike most students of these later days the Prince spent more hours in reading and writing after, than before, the period of regular tuition. In fact, Prince Rama Varma continued a scholar all his life. The large library he has left behind, embracing, as it does, a variety of well-thumbed volumes in every department of thought, would bear ample evidence of the extent and thoroughness of his scholarship. For composition, the Prince had a special bent, and aspired to distinction in it. His first attempt was an essay on 'the Horrors of War and Benefits of Peace,' written in the days of the Crimean war, and General Cullen, the then British Resident and himself an eminent scholar, was able to pronounce an encomium of which any student of the Prince's tender years might really be proud. This was in 1855. Thus encouraged, the Prince next tried his apprentice hand in the leading papers of the day. The best journal of the time in Madras was the *Athenæum* chiefly conducted by that well-known friend of the people Mr. John Bruce Norton. The first contribution of the royal essayist that appeared in the paper was 'a Political sketch of Travancore.' The editor acknowledged it as a truly valuable communication. A close and lasting friendship followed, and contributions to public prints became more or less a frequent occupation with the Prince. But such literary pursuits did not preclude attention to scientific and more solid subjects of study, as they in some cases unfortunately do. The Prince's love for the experimental sciences was too genuine to be so alienated by the charms of light literature, and he continued his studies of astronomy, experimental physics, and chemistry as ardently and vigorously as ever, adding in later years the Natural History sciences and especially Botany.

Meantime, the Prince had to mourn several deaths in his family. In 1853 died his grand aunt, Parvati Ranee who had been more than a mother to him. In October 1857 his only sister Lakshmi Bai, breathed her last just eleven days aftor giving birth to a son, the present Maharaja. In 1858, he lost his much revered and dearly beloved father to whom he attributed all that was good and great in his moral character. In the following year, the Prince having attained his twenty-second year married a lady of his own selection, from a family from which more than one of his ancestors had chosen partners in life.

In the interval the country itself had undergone a remarkable change of administration. In

December 1857, Dewan Krishna Rao died and Madhava Row was appointed in his stead; and General Cullen, the British Resident was succeeded by Mr. Francis Maltby, than whom an abler British representative Travancore has scarcely had. Reforms were in urgent need in the country and the reformers appeared in the persons of Messrs. Maltby and Madhava Rao; and heartily did they fall to their work. In all their noble endeavours, they found in Prince Rama Varma an able adviser and friendly critic. In issue after issue of the *Indian Statesman,* then edited by Mr. J. B. Norton, there used to appear under the *nom de plume* of "Brutus," stirring letters with the heading of "Topics for Mr. F. N. Maltby," which created no little sensation in those days, and which Mr. Maltby himself gladly welcomed. These public utterances of the Prince often saved the Government from unnecessary complications, such for instance as the political embroglio created by certain over-enthusiastic Missionaries in South Travancore. A pamphlet addressed by the Prince about this time to Sir George Clerk, defending the State policy of religious neutrality in Public Instruction, still worth reading and so too is another, addressed to Mr. J. B. Norton, on the educational value of Sanskrit literature. But so far as the administration of Travancore was concerned, such literary support of the Prince was not long needed. The change in the Residency was followed by a change on the throne itself. In 1860, His Highness Martanda Varma died, and was succeeded by His Highness Rama Varma an elder brother of the Prince, and a quondam pupil of Madhava Rao. Extraordinarily intelligent, and amiable to a fault, the new sovereign had an instinctive power of accommodating himself most gracefully to any society or circumstances. He afforded, therefore, ready support to all the measures of reform initiated by Messrs. Madhava Rao and Maltby: and the consequence was that in the short period of ten years, the country rose from positive insolvency to financial exuberance, from the danger of annexation to the enviable position of a model State in the Empire.

Satisfied with the bright prospect now before his country, Prince Rama Varma sought permission to put the finishing touch to his own education by travels, which his enlightened brother on the throne readily granted. The first use he made of this permission was to visit the Presidency town of Madras about the end of 1861. This was no small achievement in those days for a prince of the Travancore Royal Family. He was the first of that house to see a British satrap in his own quarters, and such was the impression he made upon Sir William Denison, the then Governor, that the latter wrote to Mr. Maltby to say: "He is by far the most intelligent native I have seen; and if his brother (the Maharaja) is like him, the prospects of Travancore are very favourable." In recognition of this fact Rama

Varma was forthwith appointed a Fellow of the Madras University—a rare honor again in those days for natives of the soil. He made at the same time a large circle of friends, including the Governor and some of his Councillors, with whom he then kept up an unremitting correspondence. This first essay at travelling was followed by almost incessant peregrinations in his own country and there is scarcely a mountain, a river, or a waterfall in Travancore, that he has not seen. The curious minded never come across a ruined temple, a worn out inscription, or a decaying fort, or other passing land-marks of history, without being reminded by the village folks that the object had already come under the observation of *Visakham Thirunal* the name by which the subject of our sketch is still known in the country. From each of these tours he would return loaded with large collections of plants and seeds, ferns and orchids, stones and minerals, butterflies and moths, stuffed birds and sundry reptiles, besides excellent sketches of landscapes and innumerable drawings of indigenous medicinal herbs, flowers and berries, executed by the artists in his own employ. Selected specimens from these interesting and ever increasing collections, he was in the habit of exchanging for others with such eminent naturalists as Sir Joseph Hooker of the Royal Kew Gardens, Drs. Anderson and King of Calcutta Colonel Puckle of Bangalore, Dr. Thwaite of Ceylon, and Dr. Bennet of Australia.

His scientific taste was never divorced from

practical application. A botanist of considerable experience as he was, he had a special aptitude for agriculture. No one who has visited the *Vatakke Kottaram* (Elia Raja's Palace) of his days—a place of his own construction in which he spent the major portion of his life—can ever forget the aspect it always presented of a busy experimental farm full of odd and original contrivances. To him Travancore, will feel ever indebted, if for nothing else, at least for the introduction and extension of the Tapioca cultivation which is fast spreading through the length and breadth of the land. Many an octogenarian in out of the way places in Travancore may be heard to-day proudly extolling the many virtues of this edible root, which, in his youth, was as rare as a white crow, but which he now considers as indispensable to his daily dinner, as the limpid waters of the neighbouring stream. When that stream gets unusually dry, and gaunt scarcity strides athwart, the sturdy cottager who elsewhere is the first to feel the pinch, boldly defies the unwelcome visitor, so long as the moisture of his naturally damp atmosphere is able to support his Tapioca plantation in the new clearings around. The poor man's food *par excellence* now in a large portion of Travancore is the esculent tubor of the Tapioca plant; and there is no poor man in the land who eats it without silently blessing the memory of *Visakham Raja* for it, though in common with his classmen elsewhere in this continent, he might know as little of his Politics, as of his Botany, and care even less for it. Impressed with the eminent value of the plant *Jatropha Manihot*, as a reserve to fall back upon in times of famine, the prince even went tc the extent of drawing the attention of the Madras Government to the necessity of widely encouraging its cultivation but with what practical results, it is not yet known. Diverse other exogenous plants too *e. g.*, Manilla Tobacco, he tried to introduce into the country, and though his own experiments were more or less generally successful, their regular cultivation has taken no root in the land.

Among the Fine Arts he encouraged were notably painting in oils and water colours, ivory and wood carving, and Damascene or kuftgari work, in all of which, especially the first, the young men he trained up have since attained considerable fame for proficiency. But, reading and writing all along took up the lion's share of his attention. His reading was of the widest description, embracing in its range the gayest as well as the gravest. There are many who still remember with pleasure the apt remarks with which he used to delight and edify them in his private conversations, dwelling now on Tennyson's 'In Memoriam,' and then on 'the Autocrat of the Breakfast Table.' His style in consequence became day by day more and more refined and natural. At first, he was an ardent admirer of Lord Macaulay, and the literary 'cunning' of that master may be traced in his earlier productions. But his fondness for stilted periods soon gave way to a more accurate and less ornate style, which resulted as a mental sedimentation from the wider and more judicious reading of his later life. His lectures on "Human Greatness" "The Relation between Nature and Art," "Our Morals," "Our Industrial Status," and the rest, as well as the descriptive pamphlets on the unique *Murajapam*, *Tulabharam* and *Hiranyagarbham* ceremonies are samples of his later style, which for elegance of language and independence of thought, are well worth reading.

Meantime circumstances led to the retirement of Madhava Rao from Travancore: and as an affectionate and grateful pupil, Prince Rama Varma sent up to the *Calcutta Review* a long and appreciative article under the heading "*A Native Statesman*" which appeared anonymously for obvious reasons. The article was universally applauded, and it was mainly through it, that Lord Northbrook's attention was drawn to Sir Madhava Row, when Maharajah Holkar desired the Government of India to choose a competent person to be entrusted with the task of administering his affairs. But at home, it was taken to smack of partizan spirit, and led to a gradual estrangement between the two brothers which, with varying degrees of bitterness, lasted till the end of the reign in 1880. It reflects, however, the highest credit on the good sense of both, that differently constituted as they were, they never allowed to the last their want of cordiality to appear as anything like open rupture. But the unfortuuate circumstance led to the rapid decline of the Prince's influence on the administration of the day though outside Travancore, his labours were fully appreciated as indicated by the offer of a seat in the Imperial Legislative Council as a non-offiaial member, by the Viceroy which the Prince was forced to decline on the score of ill-health. With Mr. Seshayya Sastri who succeeded Sir Madhava Rao, personal friendly relations, no doubt, subsisted, but he too found it necessary to retire on pension after five years' sound and unostentatious administration. Mr. Nanu Pillai, an experienced native officer of the land, was then appointed Dewan, but during the three years of his financially prosperous administration, the Maharajah may be said to have been his own Prime Minister. This was also the period when the political influence of the Prince was at its lowest ebb in Travancore.

In 1874 he fell seriously ill and his life was more than once despaired of. But despite all unpleasant surroundings and bodily afflictions his intellectual activity remained the same. Old students of the Trivandram College might still remember the gaunt appearance of the Prince, as he used to come out of his sick bed to help forward the cause of their "Debating Society" with those telling lectures of his. Struck with the extreme paucity of good reading books in Malayalam, he heartily helped the Book Committee, organized during the administration of Sir Madhava Rao, and supplemented their publications with neat little tracts and treatises on such homely subjects as 'Truth' 'Education,' 'Health,' and 'Good Deeds.' He took great interest in Industrial and Agricultural Exhibitions, and contributed to several of them in Europe and India. At the Vienna International Exhibition, he obtained two medals—one for fibres and the other for old Indian Surgical instruments. He received a gold medal at one of the Madras Agricultural Exhibitions for the best sample of Indian Coffee. In the way of illustrating the dignity of labour and the wisdom of self-help and so correcting a weakness in the Hindu character, he worked a coffee estate in the Assambu Hills, which he had conjointly started with Sir Madhava Rao. His leisure moments he delighted to spend with intellectual men. He invited humble but promising students in the Trivandrum College to the Palace for the simple pleasure of associating with and encouraging them. Several now in the higher grades of the Travancore service found in him their first patron.

Outside the country, we have seen already how sincere and steadfast was his esteem and admiration for Sir Madhava Rao. Ramiengar was another early friend of his, and we shall see presently how staunch that friendship proved. There were scores of other intellectual men in the British Service, in whose progress in life the Prince evinced deep interest and genuine sympathy. For instance, it is not perhaps so well-known that Mysore owes her first and great Dewan after the rendition, Mr. Runga Charlu, to Prince Rama Varma of Travancore, on whose recommendation his old and intimate friend, Mr. Bowring, the Chief Commissioner first took him into the Mysore service.

But the time was now fast approaching for him to appoint his own Minister. About the beginning of 1880, his brother on the throne was seized by a fatal disease, which, neglected and trifled with, soon assumed a critical aspect. In May of that year, His Highness was confined to his sick bed, from which he never rose again. On the 17th June following, Prince Rama Varma was installed on the throne of his ancestors as Maharaja of Travancore. Never did a Maharaja ascend the musnud with more universal applause. The British Resident wrote on the occasion. "I am firmly of opinion that few Princes have ever succeeded to a throne with more opportunity of earning a great name, and if your Highness devotes your talents in singleness of purpose to the good of your subjects, as I believe you will do, the benefit will not be confined to Travancore, but will be reflected far and wide over Hindustan." Mr. MacGregor rightly added: "In saying this, I do not adopt the mere ordinary courtesy of court language; but I express an opinion for which the strongest ground has been afforded by your Highness' former career and known attainments and principles." In this opinion, he was not surely singular. All Southern India entertained the same view; and every one who ever knew the Prince turned his eye upon Travancore, expecting the grandest of results from the rule of one, so eminently intelligent and erudite. In Travancore too, expectations were exceptionally high-pitched. "Happy is the country," said Plato, "where the philosopher is the king or the king is the philosopher,," and the people of Travancore were somehow of the same conviction. The new Maharaja was more than aware of the expectations formed of him at home and abroad, and felt himself even embarrassed by them. To an intimate friend of his, he wrote:—"A feeling of despondency comes over me when I think what great expectations are based on this one frail life." His thrilling installation speech breathes the same sense of oppressive responsibility. He was indulging in no oratorical flourish, when he said in reply to an address in Tinnevelly, "Ever since it has pleased God to place me on the throne of my ancestors the cardinal maxim which I have ever endeavoured to impress upon myself is '*To live for my people.*'" Sincerity, even to the extent of bluntness, was an unmistakable feature in His Highness's character, and it is impossible to suppose that he ever did anything, whether as Prince or Maharajah, which he did not at the same time believe, according to his lights, as the very best under the circumstances.

The first acts of his reign were such as were meant to rectify some of the wrongs done in the previous reign as for instance, the recalling from exile of Mr. Kerala Varma, C. S. I., the *Valiyakoil Tampuran*—Consort of the Senior Rani—an erudite scholar like himself. Mr. Nanu Pillai was pensioned and His Highness appointed Mr. Ramiengar as Dewan. This gentleman, the Maharajah knew for twenty-one years previously, and his kindred nature in certain respects had won for him His Highness' regard and esteem. The one leading feature of the Maharajah's administration was Reform. Department after department was taken up and reorganized—the Judicial, the Revenue, the Police, the Salt, down to the Anche, and the Elephant; and in spite of the clamours of the time, who can now say that each was not left behind, on the whole either better ordered, or better manned? Unseemly haste or occasional harshness was unavoidable with the conjunction of two such characters as the Maharaja and his Minister. But the captious critic must remember that His Highness was always apprehensive of his life. On one occasion he wrote: "I am myself forty-six years. None of my predecessors after the old Rama Raja saw his fiftieth year. Never put off till to-morrow what can be done to-day." Taking all in all, we have not the slightest hesitation in pronouncing the reforms of the reign to be of the soundest and the most solid description.

Besides reforms and reorganizations, the reign witnessed the inauguration of several new schemes of which the Revenue Survey and

Settlement will always stand as the foremost. In importance and magnitude, it far surpasses any administrative measure ever undertaken since the consolidation of the State into its present form. The initial difficulties of the step were equal only to the urgency, all along felt for it. Travancore is remarkably a land of small holdings, and her revenue system, like the English Common Law of Pre-Benthamite times, is a dissolving mass of the *debris* of ages. The curious tangle of anachronisms, known as her land tenures, is sufficient to perplex and overawe the boldest of Revenue Reformers, and for years together a scheme of Revenue Settlement was more talked of than attempted. But the new Maharaja with his characteristic courage and earnestness was determined to carry it out, and the well-thought out measure is now being worked, so far as it has gone, with evident profit to the State. Another measure of great importance adopted early in the administration was the Settlement by arbitration of the long-standing boundary disputes with Cochin, which, with better powers of friendly accommodation, might have ended more favourably to Travancore than they actually did.

But all these reforms and new schemes were in one respect nothing by the side of the personal influence of the Maharaja on the general service of the State. On the day His Highness ascended the throne, even the ignorant huntsman in the far-off hill tracts suddenly awakened to the consciousness that of all public sins, corruption was the most execrable. Bribery, like adultery, is always hard to be discovered, and harder still to be proved; but once the least scent of it floated to the throne, nothing on earth could shield the offender from sovereign wrath. Equally ready was His Highness to recognize merit wherever found. In earnest and indefatigable application to business, he was a model for the whole service to follow. It is doubtful whether any member of that service was harder worked than the Maharaja on the throne. His daily routine was a routine of incessant labour. Scarcely any lamp in the town was put out later in the night, or lit up earlier in the morn, than the reading lamp on the Maharajah's writing desk. Bundles of drafts passed by that carping critic, Dewan Ramiengar, would every day reach the palace by seven in the evening, and before dawn, they would be on their way back to the *Huzur*, with apt corrections and admirable amendments. On the heels of these hurrying to the post, would be found heavy private covers addressed to all the quarters of the globe. The rising sun would find His Highness himself out on his morning drive, which occasionally would appear as botanical excursions as well, from the nature of the commodities following him to his palace. After the daily ablutions, prayers, and ceremonies in all of which His Highness had such unbounded faith as to risk even his own delicate health by observing them, he would be ready again for business at about 11 A. M. The affairs of his own palace and of the temple and other establishments attached thereunto, not excluding the minutest details, would then occupy his attention till the clock struck two announcing the time for coffee. Official reports and visits would take up the remaining hours of the day; and the evening would bring on its usual round of rituals. With unerring punctuality was this routine repeated day after day. Extraordinary occupations, such as a Governor's visit, the temple festivals, or public dinners, would encroach only upon his hours of rest.

For upwards of twenty-five years, His Highness was in the habit of recording his impressions and important transactions of the day in a diary, and even after those transactions became as wide as the whole State, the diary was regularly filled before the bed was reached. It was no doubt due to the regularity of his habits and the way in which he apportioned his time that despite this heavy unfailing routine, His Highness was able to pen so many masterpieces of memoranda on general Departmental Reforms of the State, and even on such special and professional topics, as the Artesian well attempted in front of his palace. And what is more remarkable, time was found also for continuing unabated his old habits of reading and writing. In the midst of formal and business visits, he would occasionally surprise the scholarly among them by his apt observations on the latest books in their own lines of reading. He also found time to write Malayalam works. He selected from "Maunder's Treasury of Biography" the lives of some of the great and good men and women of all ages and countries, and translated them into easy Malayalam, with the hope of introducing the work into the Vernacular Schools, and thereby "nourishing," in his own words, "any sparks of noble and virtuous feelings which may naturally exist in the hearts of our youths, by holding out to them good and great examples." A condensed translation of the article on 'Astronomy' in the Encyclopœdia appeared from the royal pen in a Malayalam Journal, started under his own auspices with the name of '*Vidya Vilasini*." In English, we need allude to only the paper addressed to his friend Sir M. E. Grant Duff entitled 'Observations on Higher Education,' to illustrate how His Highness continued his literary labours even while on the throne.

His passion for travelling also asserted itself, although as observed in his reply to a public address presented to him at Alleppey in 1884, "so far as his power to carry out his inclinations in such personal matters, went, he was decidedly at a disadvantage, compared with his position five years previously." Nevertheless, in those five years he travelled a good deal. On the 26th January 1882, he started on a long tour to Upper India and returned to his capital only on the 22nd March following, after visiting the Presidency towns and other important cities like Poona, Allahabad,

Benares, Patna, Jabalpur and Indore. At most of the stations he halted, he received very flattering addresses from the public to which His Highness replied in his usual genial style. More than once during this tour, His Highness evinced his deep interest in education, by presiding at prize distribution ceremonies. One of these was at the Kumbaconum Provincial College, where His Highness after distributing the prizes delivered an eloquent and impressive speech dwelling ou the need of continued Government support for Higher Education. In 1883 he had again an occasion to visit Madras. Then was the holy trip to Benares religiously completed by a visit to Ramasvaram. Of the curious Ramasetu he wrote thus:—"I crossed the channel this morning with Capt. Howlett. I saw the venerable Ramasetu. Indeed, whether natural or supernatural, it is really a most remarkable object—a perfect straight line and of uniform width. Further, it connects the nearest points on the mainland and the Island." Within his own dominions he moved about more freely than it is usual for Maharajas to do.

Unabated too continued his love for the Arts and Industries of the land, which he took every opportunity to encourage. Having visited as a prince almost every place of note in Travancore, he had in his diary the name of the villages where any special art or industry thrived, and the names of persons who cultivated it to marked proficiency. As occasions required, he took care to command their services for the sake of encouraging them. By way of illustration, we would cite here but one such case. In the village of Armulai in the interior of Travancore, a family of smiths followed the art of polishing metals, and an old woman of the family had carried her practice to such perfection that the metallic surface under her patient hands rivalled the polish and brilliance of glass. One day a royal writ issued from the palace to the Tahsildar of the taluq, mentioning this woman by name, and ordering certain metallic pendants to be prepared by her, for the lamps of a new design, then being made for the temple at the capital. With the object of conserving and giving a new impetus to the industries of the land, a good Industrial School was started, which, with suitable improvements, might develop into a regular Technical Institute.

Of equal, if not greater, industrial importance, was the direct encouragement given for the starting of the Cotton mills at Quilon which he personally opened on the 16th December 1884 and which are still working well. Through his commendation was floated also a company for paper manufacture at Punalur, which, it is said, with better management, might have now been no less successful. The extension of the Railway to Quilon and the construction of a harbour at that port were other grand projects of industrial and commercial significance, seriously contemplated though not executed.

His Highness' deep interest in science continued also as lively as ever. Having experienced in his own person the advantages of a sound training in the experimental sciences, His Highness instituted a new chair in the local College for the teaching of Chemistry and Physics. Even better evidence is afforded of his living interest in science, by the careful records he has left behind, of his continued observations of the phenomena around him embracing alike the comet in the sky, and his own quaint dreams in sleep. For instance, he was one of the very first to notice the strange bluish tinge of the rising and setting sun in the second week of September 1883. Calling attention to this, he wrote thus to an intimate friend of his :—"Do you observe the strange light bluish tinge and absence of glare in the rising and setting sun since these three or four days? I noticed it first on Monday morning, and immediately telegraphed to Mr. Pogson of Madras."

The scientific societies of Europe were not slow to recognize His Highness' tastes and to shower honours on him. He was already a Fellow of the Madras University. The old Linnean Society of London elected him now a Fellow, which in justice to his botanical studies, they might have done full fifteen years before. In appreciation of his predilections for travels and his minute geographical knowledge of Travancore, the Royal Geographical Society recognized him also as a Fellow. He became a member of the Royal

Asiatic Society of Great Britain and Ireland, in virtue of his Sanskrit knowledge and his researches in ancient Indian surgery and other antiquities. The Statistical Society of London also owned him as a Fellow for the interest he took in the subjects falling within their scope. Even foreign European Powers delighted to honour him. The French Government of the day admitted him to the order of *Officier de l'Instruction Publique.* He was subsequently made *Member de la Societte des ettute Colonial a Maritime Paris.* But long prior to all these, Her Majesty the Queen-Empress recognized his merit by investing His Highness with the "Knight Grand Commandership of the most Exalted Order of the Star of India." The news having been telegraphed to the Madras Governor, Sir M. E. Grant Duff sent him the following significant reply:—"I warmly congratulate you and the Order." Though the honor was conferred very early in 1882, the investiture ceremony took place only on the 1st of February in the year following.

At home, too, His Highness duly qualified himself for the honorific title of *Kulasekhara Perumal* usually applied to the reigning sovereigns of Travancore, by performing the grand *Tulapurushadanam* (being weighed against gold.) It was his intention to go through the other religio-state ceremonial called *Padmagarbham* (passing through a golden cow) the next year and to make himself fit for the title of *Kiritapati;* but he was not spared to carry out the fondly cherished wish. Touching these formal rites, His Highness wrote thus:—"These ceremonies may be viewed as anachronisms in this age, but as long as one continues to be in the midst of a whole body of these, and rightly or wrongly believes in them there is no good in half-performing and half-condemning them." Somehow or other, His Highness seems to have had sincere faith in their religious efficacy, and performed them with obvious zeal and punctilious piety. Nevertheless, His Highness seems to have always entertained very broad conceptions of religion. Referring to Colonel Olcott's endeavours, he wrote:—"I am doubtful if the time has come for our B. A's to learn *Yoga Vidya* and how far they can interpret the true spirit of the Sanskrit lore. Buddha, Sankara Charya, Jesus Christ, Mahomed—all these first trained up to high standard a small but chosen band of men, and *with them* went forth to the religious battle. Colonel Olcott should adopt that plan, if he would at all achieve success." Again in another connection, he observed:—"A human *Guru* is surely necessary to *many* but not to all. My *Guru* is he that alone *ought to be Guru*. I say solemnly that I have derived great light from *Him*, when I have honestly sought it. I don't deny the great advantage of books and men of wisdom, but whenever I hear anything on *Adhyatma* (spiritual subject), I put it to the crucial test of *His* silent teaching. Revelation whether in reference to Hindu *Rishis*, or Christian prophets or others, is simply this inner teaching by Him.

In some cases, this teaching has been more vivid and effective and in others less so. But every human being, if sufficiently earnest, may reasonably hope to receive it."

It was in the hope of receiving such spiritual guidance, that the Maharajah practised with remarkable earnestness and ardour, the religious austerities—fasts and prayers recommended in Hindu treatises on piety. It is only those that have closely studied this austere side of His Highness' life that can appreciate the pardonable pride with which he speaks of himself in one of his letters, as *Rajyasrama Muni*—a hermit with a kingdom as his hermitage. He goes on to add in the same letter, "If God gives me sufficiently long life, I may become *Vannyasrama Muni*"—a hermit in the forest. But alas! The cruel hand of Death snatched him away just after the completion of the fifth year of his reign. About the end of July 1885, His Highness fell ill, and on the evening of the 4th August 1885, his soul quietly passed away. Well did His Highness remember the *Sloka* he used to quote with such approbation, meaning, "He who is conscious of having done his duty welcomes Death as a dear guest." For, whether taken as a private individual, a junior Prince, or a ruling Maharaja, his life was a life of duty done, and done with all his might and main.

SIR VIZIA RAMA, K. C. S. I.,

LATE MAHARAJAH OF VIZIANAGRAM.

His Highness Mirza Sri Vizia Rama Gajapati Raj Mannea Sultan Bahadur K.C.S.I.. late Maharajah of Vizianagram, was descended from the Ranas of Udaipore, one of the ancient and illustrious Rajput families in India. The exact date when the remote ancestor of the Vizianagram House separated from his relatives in Udaipore is lost in antiquity; but tradition says that centuries and centuries ago, one of the brothers of the then ruler of Udaipore emigrated to Oudh and made large conquests. In the sixth century one of his descendants, not satisfied with the extent of his territories in the north procceded to the Deccan and conquered that portion of Southern India extending from Ramnad to Cuttack. His successors were in possession of this territory for nearly a thousand years. Later on, in the middle of the seventeenth century, we find that another ancestor of the Maharajah was appointed "Soobadar" of the Northern Circars and presented by the Emperor of Delhi with a 'zulficar' or two edged sword which furnished the device of the Coat of Arms still used by the Vizianagur House. His son succeeded in adding ten *purganas* or baronies to the territory already acquired; and his grandson in his turn conquered the dominions of the Nawab of Chicacole and was honored with the title of "Munnea Sultan." It was this Prince who established Vizianagram as his capital and erected a Fort in that town. Under successive rulers, the dynasty was considerably strengthened and we find that at one time not less than seventeen small Zemindaries were tributary to the rulers of Vizianagar. In 1778, when Sir Thomas Rumbold was Governor of Madras, the throne of Vizianagar was occupied by Vijiaram Raja. He was succeeded by his son Narain Baboo who was held in high esteem by Lord William Bentinck. Narain Baboo died in 1845 and was succeeded in his turn by his son the late Maharajah.

Prince Vizia Rama was born on the 7th August 1826. His early years were passed in Benares where his father spent the greater part of his life. He acquired an excellent education under European tutors and was a thorough master of European manners and etiquette. As a sportsman and a rider he had few equals and he took a deep interest in all manly games. On the death of his father, he was but nineteen years old and though he inherited his estate at once, His Highness was engaged during nearly the next seven years in acquainting himself with the needs of his Zemindari and the methods of administration rather than in administering the estate himself. During this period he had the able assistance of Mr. F. H. Crozier of the Madras Civil Service, who in 1852 handed over the estate to his complete management, free from debts and with a surplus of about a lakh of Rupees in the Treasury.

For thirty years, the Maharajah was in charge of his Zemindary and it may be said without exaggeration that he lived and died a model Prince. To those who are acquainted with his life, three features strike as most prominent. First, in the administration of his estate, he was economical without being penurious and liberal without being profuse. In the second place, charitable by nature his charities were all well-directed. Thirdly, though a Zemindar he took a deep interest in all matters affecting the welfare of the public. It may be considered fortunate that though his Estate when he inherited it was encumbered with debts, he was in possession of a surplus of one lakh of Rupees when he actually took possession of it. Nevertheless, if he was extravagant, careless or thoughtless like several Zemindars of these days, whose names will readily spring to the lips of the reader, the surplus would have disappeared in no moment and his Estate would have been plunged in debts. Our surprise is how he not merely steered his estate free of such dangers, but succeeded in leaving a surplus of fifteen lakhs of Rupees at his death, particularly after his numerous private charities and public benefactions. As one who took a deep interest in the concerns of the Empire he was very often called away to Calcutta and Madras, but wherever he was, whether at Calcutta or Madras or Benares, he superintended the administration of his Estate so carefully that the Indian financiers of these days who indulge in sweet but unprofitable dreams of a surplus balance sheet, will do well to take a leaf from his pages.

The Maharajah was also a philanthropist. His charities were confined to no particular caste or creed; nor were they restricted to India. And more than all, they were always well directed. To this day, there are numerous men who are the happy recipients of such charities perpetuated by a dutiful son. It is impossible to give a complete list of his charities but a few among them may be mentionod. In his own raj, he spent lakhs and lakhs of rupees in roads, bridges and useful buildings. He established a High School, which is now a First Grade College, a Sanskrit Seminary, a school for Caste Girls, a School of Arts and a grand Market in memory of the Prince of Wales' visit to India. In Madras, he opened five Girls' schools and erected a handsome fountain which is called after him. He presented Benares with a Town Hall in honor of the Duke of Edinburgh's visit, a Library called after Mr. Carmichael, a Dispensary called the Vizianagur Dispensary, four Girls' Schools and a Racquet Court. Allahabad is indebted to him for the princely gift of one lakh of Rupees to the

Muir College and a clock tower. Several students were offered scholarships for the prosecution of their studies in Colleges established at Calcutta, Madras, Allighur, Cuttack and Ghazipur. In Hyde Park, London, he raised a splendid granite fountain. And there were few public movements in his time which he did not assist with a liberal hand. He took part in all important public meetings and made himself conversant with all public questions. He was for six years a Non-official Member of the Imperial Legislative Council; and what is far more important, he had the honor of being the first native who ever introduced and carried through a legislative enactment. The Majority Act which has found a place in the statute book of the country is the result of his labours in the Council.

His Highness' private and public virtues made him universally popular among natives as well as Europeans. He rose high in the esteem of Government and honors were showered on him. In 1864, he received the title of "Maharajah" and was appointed a member of the Supreme Legislative Council by Lord Lawrence. He attended the Durbar held by Lord Lawrence in 1886 and was invested with the title "K. C. S. I." His personal salute of thirteen guns was also extended to the Bengal Presidency. In 1874, he received the title of "His Highness" and his name was enrolled in the list of Indian Chiefs entitled to return visits from the Viceroys of India. He was visited both by the Prince of Wales and the Duke of Edinburgh: the Duke presented him with a sword and a group photo of the Royal Family and the Prince offered him a gold medal, a ring, a sword with belt, an express rifle, an ivory whip, an album containing portraits of the Royal family and a book on polychromatic art with a suitable inscription. In 1876, Lord Lytton, offered to re-appoint him as an additional member of his Council but he declined the honor on the score of ill-health. Personally, His Highness was well known for his refined and polished manners and his courteous and gentlemanly behaviour. His commanding figure and noble presence excited admiration on all occasions when he appeared in public. He was a fine specimen of an Indian Prince. The great esteem in which he was held by all who knew him was apparent from the numerous messages of condolence that were received from Governors Maharajahs, Dewans and several other illustrious men on his lamented death on the 28th of April 1879.

RAJA SIR T. MADAVA ROW, K.C.S.I.

Sir Madava Row was born in the city of Kumbaconam in 1828. He came of a highly respectable Mahratta Brahmin family. His father, R. Ranga Row, was Dewan of Travancore, and his paternal uncle Raya Raya Raya R. Venkata Row was Dewan of Travancore and Commissioner of Mysore. The early years of Sir Madava Row's life were spent in Madras where he was sent for his education. He studied in the Presidency College, then known as the High School of the Madras University, and was one of that distinguished band, now all but extinct, who drank deep at the fountain of Mr. Powell's knowledge. Madava Row was a diligent and careful, though not a brilliant student. Mathematics and Science were his forte. He learnt astronomy on the terrace of Mr. Powell's house and delighted him by constructing microscopes and telescopes out of hollow bamboos and bits of magnifying glass. His education was over in 1846, when he took the proficient's degree in the first class with high honors.

Mr. Powell, fully alive to the merits of his pupil did not suffer him to leave the High School after taking his degree, but had him appointed acting Tutor of Mathematics and Physics under him for some time. But soon afterwards Madava Row obtained a situation in the office of the Accountant-General, and while employed here, he was offered the place of Tutor to the Princes of Travancore which he accepted. This was the first step in his long career in Native States. The Princes under his charge were the late Maharaja who was a distinguished scholar and his amiable predecessor. They have justly been regarded as the most eminent rulers that graced the musnud of Travancore in modern times and Madava Row may very properly take credit for having laboured in preparing the very ground-work of their repntation. Madava Row remained as Tutor for about four years, and was then appointed to a responsible office in the revenue branch of the administration under the Dewan. Thence he rose to the office of Dewan Peishcar and obtained great credit in the management of the Southern division of Travancore which at the time was subject to serious breaches of the peace and social tyranny and oppression. The triumph that young Madava Row achieved at the time cannct be better described than in the words of the late John Bruce Norton :—

"Within the short space of a year, Madava Row has called forth order out of disorder; has distributed justice between man and man, without fear or favour; has expelled dacoits; has raised the revenues; and his minutes and State papers show the liberality, the soundness, and statesmanship of his views and principles. He has received the thanks of his Sovereign; he has obtained the voluntary admiring testimony of some of the very missionaries who memorialised, to the excellence of his administration. Now, here is a man raised up as it were amid the anarchy and confusion of his country, to save it from destruction. Annexation, looming in the not far distant future, would be banished into the shades of night if such an administration as he has introduced into two of the districts were given to the whole kingdom, by his advancement to the post of Minister. He is, indeed, a splendid example of what education may do for the Native."

The wish of John Bruce Norton was soon realised. The administration of Travancore was at the time in the hands of a Dewan who was unable to grasp the seriousness of the situation. The Maharajah was a weak prince whose thoughts did not travel beyond the daily routine of the palace and the pagoda. His officers, with few exceptions were corrupt. Their salaries were low and in arrears for over a year. The subsidy due to the British Government remained unpaid. The treasury was empty. All commerce was suspended owing to the difficulty of transit, and the heavy import and excise duties while impoverishing the people did not enrich the State. This state of affairs attracted the attention of Lord Dalhousie who began to devise plans to bring the fair and prosperous realm of Travancore under the direct administration of the British Government.

He even went down to Ootacamund to arrange the terms of the annexation with the Government of Madras. At this juncture, the Maharajah secured the aid of Madava Row who prevailed upon the Madras Government to allow him seven years' time to improve the administration and he assumed the office of Dewan or Prime Minister in 1857. Thus, at the early age of thirty, Madava Row attained by dint of honesty, ability and industry, the highest position a native of India can aspire to in a Native State.

The most striking feature of the first few years of his administration was his great fiscal reforms. The finances of the State, were in a hopeless condition. The chaotic fiscal policy that was pursued told upon the people very heavily. The country was subject to oppressive monopolies and vexatious taxes of various kinds. The most oppressive of these was the pepper monopoly. Madava Row abolished the monopoly system and levied an export duty of 15 per cent. *ad valorem* to cover the loss in revenue. This duty was afterwards lowered to 9 per cent. and ultimately to 5 per cent. He next grappled with the tobacco monopoly. Instead of the Sirkar purchasing tobacco from contractors on its own account and selling it by retail to its subjects, Madhava Rao first permitted all dealers to import tobacco on their own account, provided they paid a certain import duty. The scale of duty was first a little high, and in consideration of its pressure, importers were allowed by the Sirkar the privilege of keeping their goods in hand,—a privilege without which the trade could never have prospered. Some time after, the duty was lowered; and a still further reduction was made later on. These light duties encouraged the growth of the import trade enormously. Having done away with these monopolies, Madhava Rao turned his attention to reforming the system of general taxation. He abolished upwards of a hundred minor taxes which, while they yielded little to the State, were vexatious to the subjects. The land-tax in one district, which he found to be excessively high, he reduced considerably, and in the middle of 1863-64, he cut down the export and import duties. In the following year, the commercial treaty between the British Government and the Sirkars of Travancore and Cochin was concluded. By this treaty, State duties on goods imported from and through British India or Cochin Sirkar territories were, with a few exceptions, removed.

As a reward for these labours Madava Row was decorated by the British Government with the title of K.C.S.I.—an honour but rarely conferred on native gentlemen. At the investiture which took place in Madras, Lord Napier, Governor of Madras, spoke in the following eulogistic terms of Sir Madava Row's work :—

" Sir Madava Row,—The Government and the people of Madras are happy to welcome you back to a place where you laid the foundation of those distinguished qualities which have become conspicuous and useful on another scene. The mark of Royal favour which you have this day received will prove to you that the attention and generosity of Our Gracious Sovereign are not circumscribed to the circle of her immediate dependents, but that Her Majesty regards the faithful service rendered to the Princes and people of India beyond the boundaries of our direct administration, as rendered indirectly to herself and to her representatives of this Empire. Continue to serve the Maharajah industriously and wisely, reflecting the intelligence and virtues of His Highness faithfully to his people."

In the same year, Sir Madava Row was made a Fellow of the University of Madras. He had thus attained the climax of his ambition in Travancore and having laboured hard for years, he looked forward to a period of administration when he might rest on his oars. But this was not to be. Evil advisers poisoned the mind of the Maharajah against him, and misunderstandings soon arose between the Minister and his royal pupil, which resulted in Sir Madava Row's resignation in 1872.

Thus closed the first chapter in the great statesman's life. He brought sunshine into a land covered with darkness. He secured the blessings of good government to a people harassed by anarchy. He obtained freedom of person and property to those who were constantly assailed by hereditary robbers. He reared costly edifices in a city covered with mud huts. He constructed various works of public utility such as roads, bridges, canals, and tunnels and put the most distant and inaccessible parts into easy communication, one with another. Forests were reclaimed, waste lands cultivated, and new industries such as the cultivation of coffee, were encouraged. Peace and plenty reigned supreme. Travancore, which when Sir Madava Row took charge of it was in hourly danger of annexation, obtained when he left it the appellation of a "Model State." In short, in the words of the late Maharajah, "What Pericles did for Athens, what Cromwell did for England, that Sir Madava Row did for Travancore."

Sir Madava Row retired on a handsome pension of Rs. 1,000 which he enjoyod for nineteen years. Leaving Travancore, Sir Madava Row remained in Madras making up his mind quietly to spend the remaining years of his life in honorable retirement. He was offered a seat in the Viceregal Legislative Council which he declined. The news of Sir Madava Row's compulsory retirement soon reached England. The late Henry Fawcett, M.P., grew indignant that such abilities as of Sir Madava should be allowed to lie dormant, and asked the Secretary of State for India if the Indian Government could not find a place for him. In the course of a speech in the House of Commons, he said :—

"Sir Madava Row administered Travancore with so much skill as justly to entitle him to be considered the Turgot of India. * * * He found Travancore, when he went there in 1849, in the lowest stage of degradation. He has left it a Model State. * * * This is the kind of man for whom we have no proper opening—at a time when our resources are declared to be inelastic, and when, if the Opium revenue failed us, we should not know where to turn for the amount required."

At this time there appeared in the *Calcutta Review* a well-written article on Sir Madava Row, under the heading a "Native Statesman" by his distinguished pupil, the late Maharajah of Travancore. That article after setting forth fully the merits of Sir Madava Row added: "Sir Madava Row is still in the prime of life, being under forty-five years, and having a good and hardy constitution. Administrative work has been almost a second nature to him. He can well be under harness for ten years more." The reputation of Sir Madava Row spread far and wide and the Indian Government urged by the Secretary of State set about providing an adequate post for Sir Madava Row. Opportunely, H. H. Tukojee Row Holkar, Maharaja of Indore, requested the Government of India to provide him with a competent officer to administer his State. The offer was made to Sir Madava Row who accepted it for two years, and assumed charge of his duties in 1873.

His administration of Indore lasted only for two years. The only noticeable feature of it beyond the construction of works of public utility was the drafting of the Indore Penal Code which was completed by his cousin and successor Dewan Bahadur Ragoonatha Row. He also wrote several minutes on the Opium question, the extension of Railways in Indore, &c., which were availed of by his successors. Sir Madava Row's engagement with the Maharajah Holkar terminated in 1874. But he was prevailed upon to remain for a year. Just at this time Mulhar Row, Gaekwar of Baroda was deposed for maladministration, and the Government of India requested Maharajah Holkar to spare Sir Madava Row's services for restoring order in Baroda. The request was, of course, complied with, and Sir Madava Row was appointed Dewan-Regent of Baroda, in 1875.

The affairs of Baroda were at this time in frightful confusion. In the words of a living writer "it was a phantasmagoria of rapine and treachery, a confusing dream of intrigue and bloodshed, where reckless aspirants for ephemeral power were continually engaged in internecine contests, unredeemed by any ennobling principle, and usually to all appearance, motiveless; except so far as motives are supplied by lust of plunder and venal self-aggrandisement. It required an iron hand and an iron will to restore order in the midst of this confusion. The iron will was Sir Madava Row's and the iron hand, that of Sir Philip Sandys Melville, Resident." The greatest difficulty that required to be surmounted in the commencement in Baroda was the revenue adminstration of the country. The revenues of the State were farmed to certain nobles called Sirdars for a fixed number of years who in their turn farmed them to certain Sowcars. These Sowcars, with the aid of armed forces lost no opportunity whatever of enriching themselves at the expense of the people. Rich and poor were alike ground to death with impunity. Plunder and oppression were the rule everywhere. Having received a consideration from the Sirdars, the Government could not, with any show of justice, resume the right of collecting the revenue. Therefore, Sir Madava Row, by special acts of State, compelled the Sirdars to sell their rights. The Sirdars, who had the Mahratta blood running in their veins would not so easily submit to a new regime. Astute lawyers quoted law and precedent and spoke of appealing to the Secretary of State for redress. But Sir Madava Row pursued his course undaunted. By dint of entreaty, intimidation and deportation of troublesome people, he succeeded in restoring order to some extent.

Another difficulty lay in the same direction. The precise position of the Sirdars in the State was not defined. They held absolute rights over land on condition of furnishing troops or money to the State whenever asked to do so, as in the days of feudalism in Europe. So long as the Sirdars had absolute control over the land, there was no chance of sound administration. Their ejectment was against all law and justice. Sir Madava Row faced this question and solved it ably. The Sirdars had evaded demands of money in former times and they were largely indebted to the State. The old records were hunted up and the Sirdars were called upon to make payments at a moment's notice of all their dues with interest for seventeen or eighteen years. Their rights were attached in default of payment. Some of them who became unruly were deported to Benares and other places. Others again were prevailed upon to sell their rights for a large consideration. Order was restored to a considerable extent in this way, but the Sirdar difficulty was not yet completely solved. A third knotty point was with regard to the standing army. The State maintained a disorderly regiment of Arabs and Ethiopians called soldiers by courtesy. They were furnished with arms and committed open ravages wherever they went. Sir Madava Row determined to do away with this needless encumbrance and succeeded in disbanding the regiment, man after man, by giving them civil employment.

Courts of law, Police, schools and libraries and a host of other beneficial institutions were organised. The services of eminent men from Bombay and Madras were secured to help in the administration. Useless taxes were abolished. Narrow insanitary alleys were burnt down, and clean rows of houses were built instead, at the cost of the Government. Foundations were laid for costly and graceful structures to adorn the city. Parks and museums were erected at great cost for the amusement and instruction of the people. "It would be false modesty," he wrote in his last Administration Report, "to disguise the fact that during these five years, our work has been exceedingly heavy and trying, for the fact accounts for our visible delays and deficiencies. It is not simply that we have had to carry on ordinary current business. We have had to investigate and decide a multitude of matters inherited by us, which in number and complexity are probably unsurpassed in any other Native State. We have had to organise the machinery of Government. We have had to carefully consider and carry out vital reforms. We have had to bring under control a vast expenditure in all its dark and intricate ramifications. We have had to rectify our relations with our numerous and diversified neighbours. In this respect, grave and embarrassing aberrations from sound principles had in course of time and neglect, sprung up, and their correction presented peculiar difficulties. We have had to bring them to the notice of the authorities concerned, to explain, to discuss, to convince and sometimes to respectfully expostulate. The extra strain thus caused has, however, begun now sensibly to diminish, and it is therefore hoped that we shall be increasingly enabled to devote our time and energies to the development of internal improvments. It must be frankly admitted that there is still abundant scope for our exertions in this direction. All we claim to have done is that we have fulfilled the primary obligations of a civilized Government."

While in Baroda, Sir Madava Row was made a Fellow of the Bombay University. He also received an invitation from the Viceroy to give evidence before the Finance Committee. But he was constrained to decline the invitation on religious grounds. In 1877, Sir Madava Row attended the Imperial Assemblage at Delhi with his royal ward and was treated with marked consideration. On this occasion the title of "Raja" was conferred upon him by the Government of Lord Lytton. Sir Madava Row continued administering the affairs of Baroda with untiring zeal and ability till 1882. He formed a Council composed of the Resident and the Heads of Departments to help him in the administration. He personally superintended the education of the young Gaekwar which was placed under the care of Mr. F. A. H. Elliot, a Bombay Civilian, Sir Madava Row himself, along with the highest officers, personally giving instruction to His Highness. The Maharajah attained his majority in 1888 and was formally installed on the *gadi* in the same year by Sir James Fergusson, Governor of Bombay. Soon, differences of opinion arose between the Maharajah and his Dewan. The latter, therefore, thought it prudent to retire from the service, having learnt to be careful from his experiences in Travancore. He tendered his resignation in September 1882 and the Maharajah gave him an honorarium of three lakhs of rupees in lieu of a pension. Thus closed the second great chapter in the career of Sir Madava Row.

Having disburdened himself of the cares of State, Sir Madava Row led a retired life in Madras till the end of his days, devoting himself to his favourite pursuits and studies. Surrounded by his large family and having a wide circle of friends, European and native, he did not find his time hanging heavily upon him. He never ceased to take interest in politics. Home and foreign journals, magazines, reviews and newspapers formed an important portion of his reading. He began to take a wider interest in social questions directing his attention chiefly to female education and remedying the evils of early marriage. He did not advocate the *sastraic* method as it is now called of social reform but stuck to the more rational, if less orthodox, view that the *Sastras* required to be considerably modified before they could be of any use in the present condition of society. Nor did he advocate extreme views. He adhered to the medium policy of minimising the evil and not of extirpating it by overhauling measures.

In 1885, at the request of Sir Grant Duff, Sir Madava Row presided over the deliberations of the Malabar Land Tenure Commission and in 1887, at the request of Lord Connemara, he delivered the annual address to the graduates at the Convocation of the Madras University. The Convocation address is important merely as reflecting the dying glimmer of the powerful lamp of genius which once illumined Southern India. In the same year Sir Madava Row joined the National Congress and was elected President of the Reception Committee at the third Indian National Congress. He spoke in favour of the resolution asking for the enlargement of Legislative Councils. During the last three or four years of his life, he took to the study of Herbert Spencer's works. He was a great admirer of that truly original thinker and some of the latest of his opinions on social and political subjects were moulded on Spencer's views of society and Government. In addition to these studies, Sir Madava Row was engaged in regularly contributing to the local newspapers. Even when actively engaged in administrative affairs he found time to contribute something to the papers now and again. In those days his contributions were of great weight. For instance, his observations on the transit of Venus in 1875, gained for him a reputation among astronomers of European fame. But in later years, his contributions lost their original weight. Under the pseudonym of "Native Thinker" or "Native Observer," tit-bits on a wide variety of subjects, from the occupation of Africa by the Germans to the way in which Hindu ladies ought to dress appeared in the local papers to the amusement of the public. Some notes evidenced depth of thinking and power of observing well worthy of the writer.

In 1888, Lord Dufferin offered Sir Madava Row a seat in the Viceregal Legislative Council, but it was doclined on the ground of old age and ill-health.

In 1889, he published a little pamphlet "Hints on the training of native children by a Native Thinker." This was a work of much practical value. It has since been translated into Marathi, Guzerati and Malayalam. He sent a small note on the German occupation of Africa to Prince Bismarck, who was so much struck with the practical nature of the suggestions contained therein, that he thanked the author in an autograph letter, causing the note to be translated into German and distributed to every German soldier. He was also of a literary turn of mind. He cultivated the study of his vernacular sedulously and acquired some reputation in it as a poet. The poems, as he himself says in the preface to one of them, are "simple, free from hard words and convey instruction to children and ladies."

The great strain put upon his nervous system in the early years brought about a stroke of paralysis, on 22nd December 1890, to which he succumbed on the 4th of April 1891, after lingering for three months. There is hardly anything of his personal character and habits which was not known to his countrymen. He was a man of the highest integrity. Not a pie of his vast wealth was ill-gotten. Being raised to a high position at a comparatively early age he was rather of a reserved and aristocratic temperament. But his manners were always characterised by a charming suavity, and bewitching politeness. He was never haughty to his inferiors or fawning to his superiors. His tastes were the very reverse of oriental. He loved to surround himself with the beauties of nature and art. His collection of pictures and art-ware is inferior to none other in Madras and his taste in such matters would not fall below that of any connoiseur. He did not trouble himself about religious and speculative questions. The world as it is with its beauties and attractions, be it real or phenomenal, was his greatest concern.

V. RAMIENGAR, C.S.I.

The late Vembaukum Ramiengar C. S. I., was born in 1826 in the town of Madras. His father was a clerk and eventually Record-keeper in the Revenue Board Office in Fort St. George during the last years of Sir Thomas Munro. Of his three sons Ramiengar was the youngest and the other two were employed under their maternal uncle Vembaukum Krishniengar, a Hindu merchant, who carried on the produce trade of the Coromandel Coast in the days of the East India Company. In early years, Ramiengar was not physically strong and was, therefore, frequently sent to his maternal uncle's village of Seevaram on the banks of the Palar, as well as to his ancestral home in the village of Vembaukum, near Chingleput, for change of air. It was hard work for the father of a large family in those days of small salaries to give a liberal education to his sons; but with the thrift and forethought of Ramiengar's mother a lady of great patience and strength of character, Ramiengar was able to obtain a good education.

In April 1841, when the Government of Lord Elphinstone established their first High School in

Madras, now known as the Presidency College, Ramiengar was one of the six students that entered the new institution first, with the barest qualification of reading and writing intelligently. The class-fellows of Ramiengar were Rajah Sir T. Madava Rao, the Statesman, Sadagopacharlu, the first Native Vakil of the High Court and the first Native Member of the Madras Legislative Council, Mr. Basil Lovery, the well-known Eurasian educationist, P. Sadasiva Pillai, the distinguished native judge who presided over the Chief Court of Travancore for several years and that most intellectual scholar, Dinadayalu Naidu, who lived a life of indifferent health and died a premature death owing to over-study and consequent mental derangement. All these six obtained their Proficients' Degree with honours, the then Head Master Mr. E. B. Powell, C.S.I., the great pioneer of the Government system of education on a secular and non-sectarian basis in Madras, having followed up the capacity and zeal of his pupils and carried them beyond the limits of instruction in the various branches of literature and science, appropriate to a College course.

It was at this stage that Ramiengar imbibed a knowledge of the sciences and acquired a taste for Physical Science and Astronomy in particular. During his school-days Ramiengar walked daily with his bundle of books all the way from Black Town to the Presidency Magistrates' Court on the Pantheon Road, where the Government High School was located during the first decade of its existence; and his companion in these walks was his cousin,

V. Sadagopacharlu. There was a sad domestic occurrence which cast a gloom on his family during Ramiengar's school-days. He lost his elder brother V. Parthasaradhi Iyengar, a promising youth who was warmly loved by all who knew him; and it became a matter of necessity that he should try to pave his own way as far as his scholastic career went, without being a burden to his bereaved parents. He studied diligently, spending the midnight oil, and earned one of the stipendiary scholarships founded fortunately at that juncture by the Trustees of Pachaiyappa's Charities in the Government High School, with a view to encourage the higher education of deserving youths. About the scholarship which enabled him to prosecute his studies without requiring the assistance of his parents he always spoke in grateful terms in after-life. When the time came for him to repay the money he had thus received, he instituted himself a scholarship for science which is offered to this day to an under-graduate, prosecuting his studies for the B.A. degree in the Pachaiyappa's College.

When Ramiengar's school-days were over, the late Sir (then Mr.) Thomas Pycroft, who at that time was Secretary to the Board of Revenue, appointed him as a Translator in the Mahratta Cutcherry, where the Sheristadar wrote his reviews of the Collector's Jamabandy reports, in the Mahratta tongue. The position of Translator in the Revenue Cutcherry gave him numerous opportunities of studying the history of the system of Revenue administration in this Presidency and prepared him for active life in the higher grades of the Revenue and Financial Departments of the Public Service. By his solid abilities and diligence he soon won the confidence of the European Collectors and Secretaries. In September 1850, he was offered by the Collector of Nellore the appointment of Head Moonshee in that Collectorate. This was accepted, and Ramiengar held the office till 1854. In the beginning of 1854, when the Department of Public Works was organized as a separate branch of the administration, he was offered the appointment of Deputy Registrar under the Chief Secretary to Government, and was employed in assisting the late Sir Henry Montgomery, not only in dealing with the papers in the Department of Public Works but also in the other Departments under the Chief Secretary under Lord Harris's Government. In the following year, Ramiengar had the choice of two appointments offered to him—one that of Naib Sheristadar in the Nellore District, and the other that of Sub-Division Sheristadar in the then newly formed Sub-Collectorate in the Kistna District. He preferred going back to his old District of Nellore, where he became the Collector's confidential adviser in matters of District administration in certain branches of public business separately entrusted to him. This office he filled till March 1857, when he was appointed Head Sheristadar of the District of Tanjore. It is worth mentioning here that, while filling this office, Ramiengar declined the office of Sheristadar in the place of the then incumbent whom the Collector wanted to retire compulsorily from the service on account of inefficiency. When leaving Nellore to take up his new appointment, the Collector, Mr. F. B. Elton, a most conscientious officer, wrote a letter to Ramiengar which concluded as follows after referring to Ramiengar's attainments and character :—" Such men are the true friends of their country, and in their several spheres do much to raise it in the scale of nations and in the estimation of all good men."

He filled the post of Head Sheristadar of Tanjore for nearly a year. He was next appointed a Deputy Collector in the same District, and he continued in that capacity to be still the Collector's confidential adviser. About the middle of the following year, 1859, he was advanced by Sir Charles Trevelyan to the place of an Assistant to the Inam Commissioner for the purpose of settling the Inams in the Tanjore District and was summoned to Madras, to confer with Mr. G. N. Taylor, the Inam Commissioner, before entering upon his new duties. While he was thus employed in Madras, he was informed by Sir Charles Trevelyan that he was expected to return to Tanjore and undertake the Revenue Settlement of an important portion of the District in the Cauvery Delta, which was then under what was called the Olungu Settlement—a Settlement which fluctuated each year with the outturn of the harvest and the ruling price of paddy. This settlement was to be converted on principles laid down by Government, into an arrangement under which the Government demand on each village and land-holder was to form a fixed instead of a fluctuating item. He accordingly returned to Tanjore, and, under the immediate orders of the Collector effected in the course of eight months, the change ordered by Government in the Olungu villages. While the settlement was in progress, Sir Charles Trevelyan, accompanied by his able Secretary Mr. J. D. Bourdillon, went on a tour to Tanjore and other Southern Districts. In Tanjore, they took occasion to scrutinize the work of Ramiengar so far as it had proceeded, and after repeated and prolonged discussions with the District Revenue Officers and with the landholders directly interested in the conversion of the Olungu, Sir Charles expressed his approval of the work already done and ordered that it be proceeded with.

Speaking at the anniversary of the Presidency College in 1860, Sir Charles Trevelyan said:— "Another Native Officer who belongs to the same class has just carried through a work of the highest consequence in the Revenue Department in the Province of Tanjore, and his sterling ability and personal integrity are highly honorable not only to himself but to the nation to which he belongs." Ten years later, in a letter to Ramiengar written at a time when the Statute regarding the extended employment of the Natives of India was passing through Parliament, the same gentleman said:— "We have reached another stage of the great question of the extended employment of the Natives of India. The Bill now passing through Parliament is based upon the just principles of dealing with the natives as we deal with our own countrymen, and appointing them to any vacant situations when they appear to be the persons best qualified for them, whether their qualifications are derived from previous employment in the public service or from the general course of an active independent life. I shall be disappointed if you are not among the first to profit by the enlarged powers conferred upon the local Governments. If you were employed in important public situations for a hundred years, you could not be charged with a more difficult or responsible task than the Olungu settlement in Tanjore. You were recommended to me for the duty as being better qualified for it than any other person, European or Native, in the Presidency, and you acquitted yourself of it to everybody's satisfaction without a breath of suspicion on your previous high character although you had the fortunes of half the provinces in your hands."

On the completion of the settlement in Tanjore, Ramiengar who had orders to join the Inam Commission, was prevented from doing so, and, at the special request of the Collector, was allowed to be retained in Tanjore as the Collector's Personal Assistant. While thus employed, he was appointed by Government in June 1860 to investigate and adjust the outstanding claims of certain Mirasidars and Contractors who had received large advances from the Department of Public Works to repair the extensive damage done to the Irrigation Works in the District by the heavy floods which had occurred in it in 1858 and 1859. This duty he performed, and he succeeded in recovering a large portion of the outstanding advances. He was also entrusted in the same year with the settlement of the village of Nallattadi in the Tanjore District which was held on a peculiar tenure by a wealthy native family in Madras, and which had long been neglected by the proprietor on account of its heavy assessment. He introduced a revised assessment with the approval of the Collector and Government. In the beginning of the year 1861, the head-quarters of the Collector of Salem, which was still at Oossoor above the ghauts, was removed by Government to Salem and the Sub-Collector who was stationed at Namkul was transferred to Oossoor. Ramiengar was selected by Government to take the place of the Sub-Collector at Namkul, being at the same time promoted to the place of a First Grade Deputy Collector and invested with the full powers of a Magistrate. He entered upon his duties at Namkul in May 1861 and remained there to the close of 1864.

About this time the Government of India introduced the Paper Currency and at their request the services of Ramiengar were placed by the Madras Government at the disposal of the Supreme Government; and he was summoned to join Trichinopoly as Assistant Commissioner of paper currency on a salary rising from 600 to 800 Rupees. He accordingly entered on the duties of this appointment in the beginning of 1865, but in the course of that year he found that there was scarcely sufficient work for him as Assistant Commissioner. This fact he brought to the notice of the Madras Government, whereupon he was drafted into the Chief Secretary's Office as the Chief Secretary's First Assistant, his place at Trichinopoly being at the same time abolished. He entered on his duties in the Government Office in January 1866 and remained there during the whole of that year. In the beginning of 1867, the office of Superintendent of Stamps fell vacant by the death of the then incumbent, Colonel Temple, and Ramiengar was selected by Lord Napier's Government to the vacant post on a salary of Rupees 1,000.

In the following year, he was appointed by Lord Napier and Ettrick as an Additional Member of Council for making Laws and Regulations. He continued to be in the Council for over twelve years and had the privilege of taking an active part in all the principal measures of legislation which came before the Council during that period. With reference to the share taken by Ramiengar in the, perhaps, two most important of those measures, namely, the schemes of Municipal and Local Fund Taxation introduced into the Council by Lord Napier's Government in the year 1870, Sir Alexander Arbuthnot, a Member of the Madras Government and the Member in charge of those Bills wrote to him in the following terms after the Bills had received the assent of the Governor-General :—"Now that they have become law, you must allow me to repeat to you on paper what I have already said to you in words, how greatly I feel indebted to you for all the valuable help and counsel you have given me throughout the whole of this affair. I believe that the two Acts have been so framed that if they are well administered, they cannot fail to prove very useful measures, and if this should be the result, it will be mainly attributable to the part which you took in the preparation of the Acts and especially in their final revision."

At a later date, speaking on a public occasion, the same gentleman, referring to the College founded by Lord Elphinstone's Government in 1841 in which Ramiengar received his education, said:—"It was during that period that there was being educated a native member of our local Legislative Council—an Institution at that time unthought of, who, I am bold to say, whether as regards the uprightness of his character, the excellence of his judgment, the honesty of his purpose or the independence of his action, has not his superior in any one of the Legislative bodies now at work in this great Indian Empire."

Ramiengar was also a Municipal Commissioner for the Town of Madras for more than eight years, and was once offered the Acting Presidentship by Sir William Robinson when he was Acting Governor which, however, he declined. In May 1871, he had the high honor of being admitted as a Companion of the Order of the Star of India. On that occasion, the Governor of Madras, Lord Napier and Ettrick, wrote to him in the following terms:—

I believe that the Insignia of the Order of the Star of India will shortly be forwarded to you by the Chief Secretary to Government in the usual official form. I avail myself of this occasion to convey to you once more my sincere congratulations on the honor which Her Majesty the Queen has been graciously pleased to confer upon you, and to assure you that my colleagues concur with me in a cordial feeling of satisfaction that you should have been selected for this mark of Her Majesty's favor so well deserved by your character, abilities, and services to this Government."

In 1873 he was called upon by Government to proceed to England for the purpose of giving evidence before the Parliamentary Finance Committee which was then sitting, but he had to decline the honor on the same ground as that of his distinguished school-fellow Sir Madava Row. Two years later, when Mr. Powell retired from the office of the Director of Public Instruction and Colonel Macdonald was called upon to succeed him, Ramiengar was appointed Inspector-General of Registration by Lord Hobart's Government. At the close of the same year, he was invited by the Duke of Buckingham and Chandos to attend the Imperial Assemblage at Delhi on the 1st of January 1876, and had the honor of obtaining the Commemoration Medal from H. E. the Viceroy and Governor-General.

Ramiengar also sat in various Committees on important public questions such as those for the organization of the Department of Public Works; for revising the Madras Municipal Act; for preparing the Report on Vaccination in connection with the Municipality; for the revision of School Books in use in the Madras Presidency; for preparing a Bill for regulating the administration of Hindu Religious Institutions; for the re-organization of the Municipal Establishments; and for revising the establishment of the Sheriff's Office, the Assay Office, and the Village Munsiffs' Regulations of Sir Thomas Munro.

When his stay in Madras became a certainty after his appointment as Superintendent of the Stamp Office, Ramiengar was at the instance of John Bruce Norton, appointed a Trustee of Pachaiyappa's Charities. As a Trustee he did yeoman service by judicious advice when he and his colleagues were involved in a suit that threatened the very existence of Pachaiyappa's educational institutions. Ramiengar did much to regulate the educational charities in particular and won for the Trust Board the confidence of the Hindu public and the respect of the European and Native Staff of Professors and Masters of Pachaiyappa's Schools. It was during his connexion with the Board of Trustees that Pachaiyappa's High Schools got fairly on the high road to improvement with the new Principal Mr. D. M. Cruickshank at the head of the institution who raised it after a time to the status of a Second Grade College. It was about this time that the administration of the late Chengalroya Naik's Estate passed into the hands of the Trustees and that effect was given to the charitable objects indicated in the will—a document full of perplexing subtleties. The Trustees of those days gratefully acknowledged the value of his experience and advice in solving those subtleties and in the administration of the various charitable bequests entrusted to their management.

In 1880, Ramiengar retired from the service of the Madras Government and on the invitation of the late Maharajah of Travancore, became his Dewan and adviser. His Highness had previously had several opportunities of forming an opinion of his administrative ability, educational attainments, practical good sense and moderation, through regular correspondence with him. His career in Travancore fully justified the late Maharajah's selection. Ramiengar was Dewan of Travancore for nearly seven years, and during this period, he thoroughly re-organised every branch of the Travancore administration. He found that the Criminal Courts were working without any law defining offences or laying down the procedure, and he accordingly introduced the Indian Penal and Procedure Codes as the law of Travancore. The Police of the country having been found to be ill-paid, ill-disciplined and generally inefficient, a regulation was passed on the lines of the Madras Police Act to reorganise the entire force. The condition of the Judicial Department received his early attention as Dewan. The litigation of the country was continually on the increase notwithstanding the introduction of a higher scale of fees, and the superior

Courts were unable to cope with the increasing work. The entire judicial system was, therefore, re-organized by increasing the jurisdiction of Munsiffs' Courts and investing them with Small Cause jurisdiction, reducing the number of Zilla Judges, raising the salary of all judicial officers, separating the Police from the Magistracy, decreasing the number of Magistrates which was unnecessarily large and increasing their powers and re-constituting the highest Court of the land on a satisfactory and independent basis.

The revenue side of the administration next engaged his attention. Here the existing arrangements were even more primitive and unsatisfactory than in the judicial branch. He, therefore, placed the revenue establishment on an efficient footing by revising both the Taluq and Division establishments, the principle observed being to reduce the number of hands and raise the salaries, as the one striking feature running through the whole of the revenue establishment was the smallness of remuneration and the want of the adaptation of the staff to the work required of it. He also effected a complete reorganization of the Salt Department, having for its object the efficient supervision of the salt works and depôts. By far the most important administrative measure introduced into the State by Ramiengar was the Revenue Survey and Settlement of Travancore. The want of such a survey was long felt and acknowledged by successive administrators. The defective character of the early surveys and the imperfect nature of the revenue accounts rendered a sound administration of the State extremely difficult and as this difficulty was increasing year by year, Ramiengar resolved to undertake a regular and comprehensive survey and settlement as the only means of remedying the grave defects in the revenue arrangements. His scheme of survey and settlement defined the extent and value of all landed estates, gave an elasticity to the revenue and perceptibly improved the public exchequer so as to facilitate all measures of progress in the "Model" State, besides being a reliable record to appeal to in every case of dispute about lands and boundaries.

Among the other measures he introduced into the State were the introduction of intramural labour into jails on a systematic plan, remission of various minor taxes which while oppressive to the people were not highly remunerative to the State, the partial or total abolition of certain measures which compelled the poorer classes to supply provisions, &c., to Government at almost nominal prices, the encouragement of indigenous industries such as the starting of paper and cotton mills and the manufacture of sugar, the introduction of a Stamp Act, the remission of assessment on coffee lands, the simplification of the export tariff by the abolition of the export duty on numerous petty articles, the holding of agricultural exhibitions, the extension of elementary education by offering grants-in-aid to the numerous indigenous schools in the country, the establishment of Normal Schools, the abandonment of the import duty on opium and last, though not least, the improvement and extension of the irrigation system of Travancore. In a word, there was no department of Government which he did not overhaul and improve. It is also worthy of remark that it could not be said that he embarked public money in any undertaking that proved fruitless.

After the introduction of all these measures, Ramiengar looked forward to a long and distinguished career in Travancore the finances of which were rendered considerably buoyant by the salutary reforms he had effected. But he was not allowed to remain there to reap the fruits of his administrative work. He continued for over a year under the service of the present Maharajah of Travancore and carried on vigorously the settlement and survey work he had undertaken, so that, when he left Travancore the settlement had been completed in two Taluqs. Two of his acts as Dewan have yet to be specially chronicled; first, his stout opposition to the rendition of the Periyar waters to the British Government on the ground of injury to Travancore interests and particularly on the most easy terms agreed to by a former administration, and secondly, his exertions to release Travancore from the obligations of a railway line from Shoranur *via* Cochin to Travancore to which the Government had pledged itself to a powerful syndicate in England.

Referring to his work in Travancore the present Maharajah observed in a letter addressed to him on the eve of his retirement:—"In accepting the resignation of your important office, I feel it due to you to place on record, the high sense I entertain of the valuable and eminent services you have rendered to the State. You have brought to bear upon the administration of Travancore all the experience acquired during a long and distinguished service under the British Government, and of association with the most prominent men in the Madras Service. Combined with a firmness of purpose and an untiring energy, you have been able to lay your plans in matured wisdom, and carry them out with vigour, undaunted by the obstacles which beset your path. I need not recount the various measures of reform you have carried out; how almost every branch of the Public Service has been improved, and how the finances have prospered and been placed on a secure footing during the last six years of your administration. Your last and greatest work, the Revenue Survey and Settlement, so full of promise alike to the public exchequer as well as to the land-holders, when successfully carried out on the lines laid down by you, will I am sure, ever remain a lasting monument of your adminstration. You have, in fact, during the past six years imparted an impetus to national prosperity the full force of which remains to be felt."

The testimony of the British Resident, Mr. Hannyngton, is equally flattering:—"On the occasion of the retirement of Ramiengar, I desire to express my high appreciation of the important services he has rendered to the Travancore State during the period of over six years' tenure of the office of Dewan. The record of his administration is before Government, and it only remains for me to express my admiration of the ability, firmness and zeal with which he steadily carried out, in the face of no little ignorant opposition, measures which experience has shown to be generally beneficial. The measures introduced by Ramiengar by which he will be chiefly remembered in the State, are probably the inauguration of the Revenue Settlement and Survey and the establishment of a sound system of Police. One very important effect of his administration which does not appear on the surface, and which I will here mention, is that under his firm administration, the general tone as well as the efficiency of the Public Service has considerably improved."

In 1887, Ramiengar retired from Travancore on pension and settled down in Madras to enjoy a well-earned repose, contemplating religious study and literary undertakings. But the hot winds of May were too strong for him and brought on suddenly a slow insidious fever, from which medical skill could do nothing to save him. It proved fatal immediately and deprived this country of the fruits of his leisure, varied knowledge and experience.

Ramiengar was passionately fond of reading and not a month passed without his importing fresh books from England or purchasing some in the local bookshops; and notwithstanding the heavy claim which his official and public duties made upon him, he was not able to forego the pleasure of reading for reading's sake for at least half an hour daily. His own pen was never idle and his letters were written in a polished and graceful style peculiarly his own. Nothing can exceed the interest of some of his letters to friends describing the country he travelled through and lived in. His descriptions though brief were in words so simple, yet so vivid. His library has been presented by his widow to the Pachaiyappa's College, where his favourite books are to be seen bearing marks of careful study. He was not an orator, but both in debate and in argument his language was polished and measured and sometimes witty.

Ramiengar was of medium height with well-set shoulders. His head showed strength as well as shapeliness. In manners he was quiet, but his intelligent eyes made up for any lack of demonstrativeness by their kind expression. He never could bear the sight of a man in pain and distress. He was sober and abstemious, studious and methodical in the despatch of business. He loved and preached order and method to all who came under his influence. He was always judicial in his tone and temperament, and deprecated extravagant and exaggerated language. Another feature of his life was that he would never take anything on trust and his private and official letters show that he always liked to have his facts and figures first. Such words as 'suppose,' 'guess,' &c.

were abhorred by him. He deprecated every description of cant and was always straightforward though never offensive. He was not a demonstrative man and was liable to be misunderstood but he cherished a warm and sympathetic heart within. In a word, he always earned the respect and regard of everyone whom he met or conversed with by his upright bearing and gentlemanly demeanour and conduct.

Ramiengar was not without his faults. His likes and dislikes were very strong, but he loved to think that he could rectify his mistakes when he discovered them. He was a strict master and judged others by a severe standard so that he not unnaturally alienated from himself the affection of several men who honestly believed that they had been treated with but scant courtesy and kindness. The more constantly such persons, however, moved with him or happened to come in closer contact with him, the better they judged of him and appreciated his goodness of heart and kindliness of disposition. Faults of judgment he committed occasionally, but it is only due to him to say that these could be counted on one's fingers. He lacked also the *suaviter in modo* in private life, though he was accessible to all in his official life. He was also sparing in kind words to his subordinates, though, to those who deserved encouragement, he always showed it by official promotion and favour.

Another feature of his character was that he relented towards those whom he had punished for misconduct. These he always endeavoured to restore to their former position, if they showed signs of repentance and good behaviour. He was, over-sensitive on a point of honour; and this often led him to the brink of resigning his official position. Though a conservative by nature, *Festina Lente* was his motto. He was the first native to keep his house in European style, to teach English and European music to the female members of his family and to invite European gentlemen to parties at his residence. He took a leading part in organising and establishing the Madras Cosmopolitan Club of which he was the first Secretary, at the suggestion of Lord Napier then Governor of Madras, for the purpose of promoting social intercourse between Europeans and Natives. And, curious to tell, it was he that first suggested and asked for the expansion of the Legislative Councils, the discussion of the Budget and Financial Statement and for the right of interpellation as early as in the seventies—privileges which took such a length of time for the British Government to grant to the people.

Ramiengar was very fond of his children, all daughters, and his grandchildren; and all of them were fond of him. He would take them into his study and keep them there for some hours engaged with picture-books and photos and interesting toys, as well as with little anecdotes of other children if not of his boyhood. His gentle, tender nature made children feel at once that he was their friend.

He used to have before him in his Travancore residence, a pictorial sheet with the words "Heaven is our Hope" printed in golden letters.

C. V. RUNGANADA SASTRI.

Calamur Viravalli Runganada Sastri, was born in a small village, near Chittur about the year 1819. His father, although extremely poor, had the reputation of being one of the greatest Sanskrit scholars of his day. Born and nursed in the cradle of poverty, Runganadam's parents were unable to give him any substantial education beyond instructing him in Sanskrit. It is said that he was extremely precocious in his youth. In his eighth year he was able to speak Sanskrit, and to construe it correctly. He was passionately fond of play, and took a delight in romping with street boys. It was the pride of his latter years that at ten he was able to scale the highest walls and climb the tallest trees.

When he was twelve years old, an incident occurred, which may well be considered as the turning point in his life, and which was destined to raise him to the ranks of the foremost men in India. His father had taken an *Ijara* of certain lands under Government. The crops having failed, and he being unable to pay the Government dues, he was according to the custom prevalent in those days, lodged in the Civil Jail. While the father was in jail, his father's annual ceremony had to be performed. Runganadam's mother, not knowing what to do, fell a crying. Seeing his mother cry, the feelings of young Runganadam were deeply agitated and on ascertaining from her the cause of her sorrow, he resolved to go to Chittur to obtain his father's release. He went to the house of the District Judge Mr. Casamajor at Chittur and laid his case before him. The Judge told him that he would not release his father, without taking security for his re-appearance. Runganadam said in reply that the only security he could give was himself, and offered to take his father's place in jail. Such an unexpected offer coming from a boy of twelve, moved the feelings of the District Judge. He at once ordered the immediate discharge of the father, and asked Runganadam to go home and see him the next morning. Runganadam himself took the order of his father's discharge to the jail authorities, obtained his father's release and reached home late in the night. His mother was surprised to see her husband return, and upon hearing that it was due to her dutiful son, she lavished on him the tenderest caresses. It was the pride of Runganada Sastri in his old age, to describe the treatment he received at the hands of his parents on that epoch-making night.

Early in the morning, Runganadam again started for Chittur, and at the appointed time was at the house of Mr. Casamajor. The benevolent

Judge received him very kindly and after questioning him about the state of his family, asked him whether he would begin the study of English if he undertook to bear all his expenses. Runganadam, like a dutiful son said that he would consult his parents before giving any reply. The Judge thereupon sent for his father and prevailed upon him to give his consent, and the very next morning Mr. Casamajor himself taught Runganadam his A. B. C. The progress made by young Runganadam was remarkable. Within the short space of six months he was able to read English correctly.

Mr. Casamajor finding himself unable to do justice to his new pupil, recommended him to the care of one Mr. H. Groves, a missionary residing at Chittur. Mr. Groves spent nearly the whole of his morning hours in educating his new pupil. Mrs. Groves also treated him with remarkable consideration. Runganadam's residence was about five miles distant from Mr. Grove's house. One morning, Mrs. Groves found him coming walking and asked him whether he had had his breakfast. Receiving a reply in the negative, she at once ordered her milkman to give him half a measure of milk every morning immediately on his arrival. This and various other acts of kindness of a like nature, were the constant theme of Runganadam's conversation in his latter years.

Runganadam evinced a remarkable aptitude for mathematics, a subject in which Mr. Groves was himself a proficient. Within two years he advanced as far as Conic Sections, and had begun the study of Astronomy, a subject in which he took the greatest interest till the last day of his life. As time passed on, the fund of Runganadam's knowledge increased proportionately. Mr. Casamajor who was bent upon giving him a liberal education, wanted to send him to Madras. At first, Runganadam's parents were very reluctant. The counsel of the Judge, however, soon prevailed, and in the year 1836, he was sent to Madras, with a letter of introduction to Mr. Kerr, the then Principal of Bishop Corrie's Grammar School.

Mr. Kerr was astonished at the capacity for knowledge displayed by his new pupil. The regard which the master had for his pupil is expressed in a book entitled "Domestic Life of the Natives of India," published by Mr. Kerr on his return to England, after a long service in India, first as Principal of Bishop Corrie's Grammar School at Madras and then as Principal of the Hindu High School at Calcutta. Runganadam used to go often to Mr. Kerr's house, and Mr. Kerr, in his book says that at such meetings, they read together *Smith's Wealth of Nations, Locke's Essays on the Understanding* and *Paley's Natural Theology*. "At what I may call our meetings for mutual improvement," writes Mr. Kerr, "we often engaged in general conversation, after the more serious business of the evening was over. I was astonished to find so little difference between his mind and that of an intelligent European. His mental powers were equal to those of any European of the same age I have ever known, while his amiability, truthfulness and manly honesty were above all praise."

During the time Ranganadam was at Madras, Mr. Casamajor took the deepest interest in his welfare. The following letter written by him to Mr. Kerr shows that the interest taken by him was of no ordinary kind :—" I really believe Runganadam to be worthy of all the culture that can be bestowed upon him and in this confidence I am desirous he should remain with you as long as you think that he is likely to add anything to his knowledge. How long this will be, no one can judge as well as yourself. I have all along wished to give you a *carte blanche* respecting him. I feel that he is in perhaps the most favourable situation for his improvement that could have been provided for him, and my only anxiety has been that he should be able to take the fullest advantage of that situation. I do not know to what extent you have acted on the authority to supply him with books, but I wished it to be understood and acted upon in a very liberal sense. He is now likely to require more and more, and I beg of you not to stint him. For instance, I have no objection to your supplying him with an encyclopædia and the best dictionaries if you think the time has come for him to use them with advantage. You need not tell him (and I had rather you did not) that the books are given him as his own, or by whom they are supplied. He will think they are yours, and so perhaps take more care of them. You may give them to him as his own when he leaves."

During the whole of the time that Runganadam was at Bishop Corrie's, not a week passed without his writing to Mr. Casamajor about the progress made by him. The following extract from a letter written by him, will show that his passion for knowledge was of no ordinary kind. "I was during the whole of last week, engaged at the rate of two or three hours a day, in writing an essay on 'Female Education.' It is rather too long. It consists of twenty-eight pages. During the time, I was writing the essay, I was led to consider when would my countrymen learn to see education in its true light, and appreciate it for its own sake, and not pursue it with the unworthy motive of making it a tool for procuring money. I clearly see that the greatest of all benefits that either a European or a Native can do for the good of this country is to disseminate the happy seeds of education."

This yearning for knowledge, for its own sake, was the pole star of his life, and it was this firm resolve which left him at the time of his death, master of fourteen different languages. When during the holidays Runganadam was in his native place, Mr. Kerr and he used to correspond with each other on the most intimate terms. The following is an extract from a letter written by him to his master: —"With sincere respect I beg leave to address you the following letter. I am detained here longer than I expected. I am now very fond of

Algebra. I worked all the problems in Hutton's Mathematics with the exception of five. My esteemed friend Mr. Groves has lent me his Algebra by Euler, and I have worked several questions in it. These I have copied in my exercise book, and hope to show them to you."

The holidays were entirely spent by him at Chittur, in going over the books in Mr. Casamajor's library. He and his patron were constantly in the habit of meeting and discussing various questions. The following letter written by Runganadam to Mr. Kerr will show how he stood in the Judge's estimation :—" I saw my generous and kind patron at his house. He received me with extreme kindness, of which it is my sincere desire to prove myself worthy. He asked me about my studies with you, and he was pleased to hear that we were reading together *Herschel's Astronomy* and *Smith's Wealth of Nations*. He asked me about my views after leaving school. I told him my views without the least reserve. I told him that I would be very glad to be employed in the projected University of Madras, and that very few situations would be so much to my mind as that of Professor in the University. I told him that I deem it my duty and feel it a pleasure to wait for his advice on the point. He concluded by saying : 'You will always find a a firm friend in me. God bless you.'"

About the year 1839, Mr. Casamajor was transferred to Madras, as Judge of the Supreme Court, and Mr. Kerr got a situation in Calcutta.

Mr. Casamajor was unwilling to allow him to remain any longer at Bishop Corrie's, and sent him to the old high school with a letter of introduction to Mr. Powell. He was soon admitted, and in a few days, Mr. Powell came to know the stuff of which Runganadam was made. The remarkable aptitude for mathematics displayed by him induced Mr. Powell to make him teach that subject to the lower class. Rajah Sir T. Madava Row was then one of Runganadam's pupils. In the year 1842, Rungandadam presented himself as a candidate for the Proficient's degree and came out with honours. He was the only one who passed that year, and his name still stands in the Presidency College Calendar, as the first among Proficients.

On taking his degree he went to see Mr. Casamajor at his house. He received him with open arms and said: "Why, Runganadam, I feel myself perfectly rewarded by your conduct. God bless you." They had a very long conversation as to his future career. Runganadam's greatest ambition was to become a Professor in the University which was about to be formed. He let slip many other opportunities, and did his best to get the desired situation. The following letter written by him to Mr. Kerr on taking his degree, shows the inclination of his mind. "During the first two years of my continuance at the High School, I had made up my mind to prosecute my studies in mathematics, and procure the situation of teacher in the projected Engineering College, and had even the vanity to fancy that I might become a Professor in the same way as Gangadhara Sastri of Bombay." Mr. George Norton who was then president of the University Committee, as well as Mr. Powell and Mr. Casamajor recommended him very highly for the coveted post. Unfortunately for Runganadam, the Madras Government smashed all the plans of the projected Engineering College. The subsequent hostile attitude of Government towards the High School gave him no hopes of getting a situation there, notwithstanding the endeavours of Mr. Norton and Mr. Powell.

When matters stood thus, Runganadam was summoned to Chittur, where his father was very ill. He wanted to obtain a footing at Chittur, to enable him to be by the side of his father in his old age, and asked Mr. Casamajor to help him to get it. The Judge was only too glad to help him. He gave him a letter to the Collector and Runganadam, a few days after his arrival at Chittur, was given the post of Head Clerk in the Subordinate Court, on a salary of Rs. 70. He had ample leisure for study, and did not let slip the opportunities he had to increase his fund of knowledge. He began the study of Telugu, Hindustani, Persian and Canarese. and the progress he made in them was remarkable. Nearly the whole of the records in Court were translated by him alone and every successive Judge was astonished at seeing the talents displayed by him. He was thrice ambitious of securing a post in the Supreme Court. His father died, and he wished to leave Chittur. Fortunately for him the post of Interpreter in the Supreme Court fell vacant, and the Judges resolved to throw the post open for competition. Mr. Casamajor wrote to Runganadam, and asked him to send in his application. This was soon done, and Runganadam offered to stand his trial in Tamil, Telugu, Maratha, Canarese, Hindustani, Persian, and English. His superiority was perfectly decisive, and the post was conferred on him.

As Interpreter in the Supreme Court, he had ample opportunities of distinguishing himself. His personal contact with the Judges made them admire the ease and fluency of his interpretations. As days passed he rose in their estimation, and their opinion of him was so very high, that they did not fail to compliment him openly, whenever there was an opportunity. Having exhausted all the languages of Southern India, he betook himself to the study of the languages of Europe. French and Latin soon opened their treasures to him. One day, the services of a French Interpreter were wanted in Court. Runganada Sastri at once offered his services, and the presiding Judge Mr. Gambier was surprised at the offer. He asked him to proceed with the interpretation, and within a few minutes, was astonished at the accuracy of his interpretations. From this day he became a personal friend of the Judges. He was invited to their house often and most of his holidays were spent in conversing upon many questions with them. The following testimonial given to him by one of the Judges, will show the estimation in which he was held by them. "I say unhesitatingly, that you are out-and-out the best interpreter I have met with. I have received your interpretations not only from many Hindoo languages, but also from those of Europe, and have never had any occasion to correct you. I must add, my unqualified good opinion of your honourable conduct as an officer of this Court."

The post of Chief Interpreter in the Supreme Court, was not the same trifling post it is now. The Interpreter was then paid by commission, and Runganada Sastri who was master of many languages was able to make between Rs. 2,000 and 2,500 a month. He was at this time a master of the Sanskrit language, and his elucidation of the texts was so very clear, that not a single intricate point of Hindu Law was decided without his opinion being given. Sir Christopher Rawlinson was his greatest admirer, and in the year 1857 when the Madras University was established, it was through his influence that Runganada Sastri was made a Fellow.

In the year 1859, when Sir Charles Trevelyan came out as Governor of Madras, Sir Christopher introduced Runganada Sastri to him as the most enlightened native in Madras. Sir Charles soon became an ardent admirer of Runganada Sastri. He was constantly invited to Government House, and with him Sir Charles discussed many questions regarding the social condition of the Hindus.

In April 1859, there was a vacancy on the Small Cause Court bench and Runganada Sastri's name was mentioned in connection with it. Much opposition was raised to his appointment on the score of his being a native. But Sir Charles was firm and the acting appointment was given to Runganada Sastri. The ability displayed by him in his new post soon falsified the predictions of those who were opposed to him. He was everywhere spoken of as a wonderful man who could distinguish himself in any capacity. He continued to act as a Judge of the Small Cause Court until 1862, and was confirmed in that appointment on the third day of February 1863. When he gave over charge of his appointment as Interpreter, he received a letter from Sir C. Scotland, and Sir Adam Bittlestone in which they said: "In acknowledging the receipt of your letter informing us of your appointment as Judge of the Small Cause Court, and tendering your resignation of the office of Chief Interpreter, we cannot but express the satisfaction we feel, at your well-merited promotion, whilst we regret the loss to ourselves of your valuable assistance, which is the necessary consequence of that promotion; nor can we permit you to retire from an office which you have filled so ably for so many years, without conveying to you an assurance of the high esteem in which you have ever been held by the Judges under whom you have served."

As Judge of the Small Cause Court, Runganada Sastri had ample time at his disposal. His shrewd common sense, and his knowledge of several languages enabled him to go through his work in a few hours. Courteous and affable to all, he is still remembered as one of the best Judges that graced the Court.

He now began the study of Arabic, a language in which he made considerable progress. *Hafiz* and *Sadi* were his favourite authors, and he took a pride in getting their best passages by heart. As time rolled on, the fund of his knowledge increased proportionately. In every field of knowledge which he entered, he walked with giant strides. He came to be lionized wherever he went, and his scholarship was the talk of the day. He enjoyed the confidence of successive Governors, and every one of them treated him with marked consideration. His Grace the Duke of Buckingham was his sincere admirer and it was he that induced Runganada Sastri to add German to his store of knowledge.

In the year 1867, Runganada Sastri was appointed a Trustee of Pachaiyappa's Charities, in the welfare of which he took a keen interest. In 1877, he was honoured with an invitation to be present at the Imperial Assemblage held at Delhi, and was presented with a medal and certificate of confidence from the Viceroy. On the 16th of February 1880, he retired on pension and in honour of his distinguished services, he was made a Non-Official Member of the Madras Legislative Council. In July 1880, he was offered by Sir Salar Jung, the post of Private Secretary on a salary of Rs. 2,500. This honor he declined, as it was his ardent desire to spend the evening of his days among his books, and in the education of his grand-children. But he was not destined to realise the objects he had in view. Death which is no respector of persons, overtook him on the 5th day of July 1881.

Runganada Sastri was in stature full six feet. The muscular development of his body was a matter of surprise to many an Englishman. Mr. Kerr says in his book,, "Of all the Hindus with whom I have become acquainted in India, perhaps the most interesting is my friend Runganadam. His personal appearance was very much in his favour. He was for a Hindu rather above the middle height, stout and well made. His complexion differed but little from that of a European well-bronzed by a tropical sun. His features were regular and even handsome, his eye bright with intelligence, his forehead one of the finest I have ever seen. The expression of his face was generally serious." In every assembly in which he was present, he was immediately recognised, and his powerful voice carried with it an amount of authority which few dared to dispute. Himself open to conviction, he always tried to convince others by argument.

The secret of his success lay in the mechanical

precision with which he went through the routine of life. His movements were like clock-work, and one merely had to see what he did—to know the time. He was passionately fond of exercise, and used to spend the first hours of the day in the building up of his physique. An ardent admirer of native gymnastics, he used to go through a regular course of training every morning between four and five. From five to seven he was on horseback, and it might be said to his credit that the firmness with which he sat on the saddle was admired by many Englishmen. The evenings were generally spent in taking long walks. Such being the training he gave his body till the last day of his life, it is not surprising to hear that there was hardly a single day in his life on which he was confined to bed. Six hours of the day were regularly spent in his study and it might be said that he was the only native who died book in hand.

Whatever he did, he tried to do to perfection. He never knew the way of doing things by halves. Himself a thoroughly conscientious man, he hated falsehood in all its forms. As a man of culture Runganada Sastri occupied a very high place in India. "I was astonished to find" says Mr. Kerr, "so little difference between his mind and that of an intelligent European. His mental powers were equal to those of any European of his age." In the evidence of Mr. George Norton, formerly a Judge of the old Supreme Court, given before the Parliamentary Committee which sat in England in 1853, he said with regard to the attainments of Runganadam. "He is a young man of very powerful mind, and would have been a distinguished man at either of our Universities. He is as remarkable for the strength and powers of his mind in mature life, as I should say almost any European." The extreme uniformity of his life, coupled with equable cheerfulness maintained by habits of regular work, enabled him to amass a vast amount of knowledge.

In style, he aimed at the simplicity and strength of undefiled English. In every language he took up, his aim was to go through the best authors. Their best passages he could repeat word for word. His library consisted of over three thousand volumes and every book bears marks of having been handled by him. The references which are to be found on almost every page to the other books in other languages, containing similar thoughts, show that his study was of the most critical kind. He took a delight in reading old authors. Cicero, Virgil, Plato and Aristotle were his favourites. His admiration for Cicero's orations was so great that he was able to repeat most of them by heart. With him, to read a passage once was to understand it, to read it twice was to be able to repeat it, and to read it for a third time was to treasure it in his mind. Arabic and Persian he could speak like the most accomplished Moulvie, and the best passages of Hafiz and Saad were always at his fingers' ends. He did not take equally great delight in English poetry. Pope and Milton were the only poets he liked. It was his firm conviction that the best of poets thrived only in the East.

He loved knowledge for its own sake. It was not in his hands a mere tool for making money. This was the idea he formed in his school-days. And it was this thirst for knowledge for its own sake which left him at the time of his death master of fourteen different languages, *viz.*, Tamil, Telugu, Malayalam, Canarese, Marathi, Hindustani, Persian, Arabic, Sanskrit, Latin, Greek, French and German and a student in a fifteenth—Hebrew. The treasures of Sanskrit literature were to him the dearest. There is not a single book in Sanskrit which has escaped his attention, and the countless manuscripts which he purchased at high prices show that his appreciation for that language was of the most enthusiastic kind. Of him it might be truly said while seated in his library :

"His days among the dead were passed
  Around him he beheld,
Where'er his casual eyes were cast
  The mighty minds of old.
His never failing friends were they
  With whom he conversed day by day."

As a Patron of letters Runganada Sastri was not behind-hand. His enthusiasm for learning showed itself in his zeal for communicating knowledge to others. His great principle was—teach or be taught. He had always around him a number of scholars in different languages, and his happiest hours were those spent in their company. He rewarded them all munificently. French and Latin, he studied under an eminent Frenchman from Pondicherry, whom he was maintaining in his own bungalow, and to whom he was paying a hundred rupees a month. To one Sanscrit pundit, for whom he had the highest admiration he gave presents amounting at times to five hundred rupees. He was always fond of educating others himself, and had in his house half a dozen students whom he fed, clothed and educated at his own expense. In the Senate, he was ever ready with his counsel and the good work done by him may be estimated by the following testimony of Mr. Norton :—"I have every expectation that he will apply his powerful mind and untiring efforts for the amelioration of the condition and prospects of his fellow-countrymen, who are already deeply indebted to him for his past labours as one of the Governors of the Madras University."

As a social reformer Runganada Sastri occupied a very high place. He was the first to point out the evils of Hindu customs and to attribute the backward condition of the Hindus to those evils. Mr. Kerr says in his book. "I remember having an interesting conversation with him one evening, on the subject of the social condition of his countrymen. He seemed to be convinced that the backward state of his countrymen, was mainly owing to a silly reverence for old customs, however absurd they might be." He worked heart and soul to efface these evils. He had however to work single-handed and was, therefore ,unable to accomplish much. He was the first among natives to wear boots and trousers though this was a small matter. At first, he was ridiculed by many of his countrymen, but being a man of iron will, he never gave up the habit. The opposition gradually grew weak, and many flocked to his standard. He was a great believer in female education. While reading at the Bishop Corrie's Grammar School, he was asked by Mr. Kerr to write an essay on female education. He wrote one twenty-eight pages long, and after strongly advocating it, he concluded as follows:—"I think it unlikely that the natives will be inclined to enlighten their females by educating them, unless the men themselves are first well educated. In all the civilized countries of Europe, the education of the females, was subsequent to that of males. Hence in this country too, the education of the males should precede that of females" His only daughter, he educated personally in Sanskrit, Tamil and Telugu. Whatever he thought best he did, and thus set an example to others.

With all these Western notions in him, he was a staunch Hindu. He was well versed in the Vedas, the Bible and the Koran, and delighted in taking part in religious controversies and establishing the supremacy of his own religion. He tried to make Hinduism suit the requirements of modern civilization, and not allow it to remain an impediment. It was through his exertions that a Brahmin boy, who was converted to Christianity, and who remained in the custody of the missionaries was rescued and reconverted. He was no great respecter of the caste system. He believed in the doctrine of *Karma* and his principle was—be true and just. Virtue, he always said had its own reward. Truth was the god he worshipped most. He is known never to have uttered a lie during the whole of his life. Even the worst of his enemies did not deny him this quality. With him, truth was everything. This sterling quality which he possessed was characteristic of him even in his school days. Mr. Kerr says in his book that while at school "his amiability, truthfulness and manly honesty, were above all praise." In a letter of introduction given by Mr. Kerr, to one Mr. Bowie, he says. "There is a highmindedness, and if you will pardon the expression, a moral dignity in the young man, that I have never seen equalled in any other Hindoo."

He had very high notions of dignity, and could not brook the idea of being insulted. In society, he was rather reserved and had no faith in too many friends. Tall talk he hated, and never mixed with every one indiscriminately. Those whom he knew, he knew well, and with them only he was intimate. His manners were those of the most polished kind, and, what provoked him most, was to find persons wanting in manners. Those who saw him for the first time, always thought that he was a very proud being but this idea was soon wiped away, when they came to know him well. He knew no two ways of treating people. He was courteous to all—Europeans and Natives were alike in his eyes. Simplicity in life was his motto, and above all, he was free from any notions of false pride. Being brought up from his youth in the society of Europeans, he imbibed one great quality which is characteristic of them—Independence. He was never known to cringe or fawn for favours at the hands of any one. He was always treated as an equal, by the many Europeans with whom he was associated. The following letter of George Norton, shows how he was esteemed by Europeans. "On, my departure from India, I am desirous of leaving in the hands of my personal friend, some testimony of my high esteem for his character and of my opinion of his distinguished and extensive attainments. I can personally testify to his superior attainments in most parts of English literature. I have every reason to believe that as a linguist, he is unrivalled in India. He has always exhibited moral qualities which must even recommend him as an honorable man, and there is no post or office to which a native can aspire, to which he would not do ample justice and honour. He has my cordial wishes for distinguished advancement." He was the first proficient of the Madras High School, the first Indian Fellow of the Madras University, the first Indian Judge of the Court of Small Causes, and the first and only Indian linguist who knew fourteen different languages.

SIR T. MUTHUSAWMY AIYAR,

K. C. I. E.

Sir Tiruvarur Muthusawmy Aiyar was born of a very poor but respectable family in the village of Vuchuvadi, in the Tanjore District, on the 28th January 1832. To his great misfortune, his father, Venkata Narayana Sastri, died while Muthusawmy was very young, and the burden of bringing up young Muthusawmy and his brother fell on the mother. With the small fortune she had, she removed to Tiruvarur, where, under her kind and careful supervision, they received a rudimentary knowledge of Tamil. But as her scanty means did not permit her to allow her sons to remain long in school, young Muthusawmy was forced rather too early in life, to seek some means of livelihood.

He became an Assistant to a Village Accountant on a salary of Re. 1 *per mensem* and while in this humble position an incident happened which shows how sensitive young Muthusawmy was. On the occasion of a Hindu festival he was presented by a relative with a new cloth. Muthusawmy thought the quality of the raiment was of an inferior kind and he accordingly indulged in some very disparaging remarks to that effect. The relative in question replied that the cloth was quite good enough for a boy depending on charity like himself; whereupon the future Judge divested himself of his garment, rent it in twain and flung it at the astonished donor. He was thus left without the new cloth which according to custom he and his relatives received at that time of the year; so he decided to purchase a cloth for himself, but unfortunately his means did not permit of such extravagance, for he used to hand all his earnings to his mother. The lad was therefore, compelled to work during extra hours in order to earn a few more annas which he carefully laid by, till he had accumulated sufficient money to procure another cloth in lieu of the one which he had indignantly destroyed.

His mother was not spared long enough to enjoy even the pittance he was able to earn. She died soon after. Her devotion to young Muthusawmy was so great that he gratefully attributed all his later success in life to the wholesome influence of his affectionate mother. It was she that inspired him with a strong love for learning to which he owes all his greatness.

Till the year 1846, he continued as the Village Accountant's Assistant. In this situation, however, he was not suffered to remain long, for he soon found a patron in Muthusawmy Naiken, who was known as "Butler—Tahsildar," presumably because he began life as a butler to Sir Henry Montgomery. This gentleman was struck with young Muthusawmy's intelligence and industry, and even foresaw a bright future for him. The way in which the Tahsildar happened to form a high opinion of Muthusawmy's intelligence and habits is testified to by the following anecdotes. One day, the Tahsildar received a report informing him of a breach in an adjoining river-belt, and being anxious to obtain some information about it, he sent for a clerk in the Cutcherry. But there being none in the office at the time, young Muthusawmy made bold to approach the Tahsildar and await orders. The Tahsildar put the report into Muthusawmy's hands and asked him if he knew anything about the breach. The boy said he would obtain the required information immediately, and taking the report with him, he went to the spot, ascertained the dimensions of the breach, inquired where the materials for its repair could be had, and in a short time submitted a written report furnishing all the necessary information. The Tahsildar, though at first not inclined to credit the report submitted by the boy, signed the paper owing to the urgency of the occasion and sent it at once to his office. Meanwhile, the Head Clerk turned up and on reference being made to him by the Tahsildar, he found that the boy's report was accurate.

On another occasion, a certain Mirasidar called on the Tahsildar to know how much his arrears of tax amounted to. He owned lands in more than twenty villages which lay scattered in the Taluq and the Tahsildar was not able to give the information without consulting his clerks. Finding, however, young Muthusawmy standing close by, he asked him if he knew anything about it; and to his surprise he received an answer which, on verification was found to be correct. These two incidents raised young Muthusawmy in the estimation of his master.

Muthusawmy, however, was not satisfied with the humble place he occupied in the Tahsildar's office. There was in Tiruvarur at that time a small primary school, managed by one Chockalingam, and young Muthusawmy having generally no work between 11 A. M. and 2 P. M., frequented the school just to see what was being done there. His repeated visits, however, enabled him to pick up in a few days the English Alphabet, and though he had a great mind to continue his studies, he was precluded from doing so by his straitened circumstances. But the Tahsildar had a nephew living in his house in whose education he was deeply interested. And in his leisure hours, he taught him and young Muthusawmy the *First English Reader*. Once, the Tahsildar allowed a week's time to both of them with a view to judging what attention each paid to his studies, and to his great astonishment he found on examining them at the end of the week that the Brahmin boy had gone through the whole book while his own nephew had read only a few pages of it. It was then that the Tahsildar realised how promising young Muthusawmy was and he resolved at once to give him a better education. He asked Muthusawmy if he would go to the Mission School at Negapatam to prosecute his studies. The boy agreed, and he was sent there and placed under the guardianship of the Tahsildar's brother. Here, he stayed for nearly eighteen months and during that period gave sufficient evidence of his laborious nature.

Soon afterwards, the Tahsildar sent him to the Madras High School, with a note of introduction to Raja Sir T. Madava Row who had just then closed his distinguished career as a student. He joined the school, and under the constant supervision and guidance of Sir Madava Row, of Sir Henry Montgomery who, out of pure love for Tanjoreans took delight in looking after the Tanjore boys then in the school and of several others, he continued his studies earnestly. Mr. Powell, who has rendered excellent service in the cause of native education in Southern India, was then the Principal of the High School, and under his tuition Muthusawmy became a "marvellous boy," winning prizes and scholarships year after year. He was regarded as clever in Mathematics and his *forte* was Astronomy. He also distinguished himself in Spherical Trigonometry.

In these days, students very rarely come in personal contact with their Professors, except in their lecture rooms; but in the days of Muthu-

13

sawmy's pupilage, students had the fortune to learn more from their masters' private conversation than from their teachings in class-rooms. Mr. Powell, while most laboriously and conscientiously discharging his duties in cultivating the intellect of his pupils, succeeded also in winning their affection. Muthusawmy had all along been his favourite boy. After the day's work in school Mr. Powell would teach him lessons in Astronomy, of which the boy was passionately fond and often detain him in general conversation till so late as nine o'clock in the night; and what is more remarkable, drive him home to Mylapore and leave him safe at home. He took such deep interest in the boy that he often audited even his monthly expenses at home.

Muthusawmy was always more studious than playful; and his studious habits enabled him to carry away some of the best prizes in the school. In 1854, the Council of Education instituted a prize of Rs. 500 for the best English Essay open to all students of the Presidency; Muthusawmy competed for it and won it. The subject of the Essay was "National vices and means to rectify them." His answer papers attracted the notice of the late Mr. Justice Holloway, who remarked: "Mr. Muthusawmy is one of those whose intellectual attainments any country may justly be proud of." Sir Alexander Arbuthnot and Mr. Holloway were then the Secretaries to the Council, and had consequently abundant opportunities to know and admire the boy in his career as a student. The reward of Rs. 500 was bestowed on him by the Council and he was gazetted as "being fit for any service under the Government." In handing him the money, Mr. Powell remarked that he hoped it would form the nucleus of a fortune which would assuredly result from the distinguished career in store for him. Muthusawmy carefully put this money aside and to his dying day did not spend a single Rupee of it.

Mr. Powell, convinced of the pupil's talents asked him if he would go to England to study for the Civil Service. But, as is the case with many an Indian youth, he was at the time married, and he could not or would not undertake the voyage. Soon after he completed his studies in the High School, Muthusawmy was employed as a tutor on a salary of Rupees sixty. He was then sent as a Record-keeper in the Collectorate of Tanjore by Sir Henry Montgomery, and this reminds us of a funny incident in Muthusawmy's life which is worthy of being related. Before securing this appointment he had seen Sir Henry Montgomery with a note of introduction and he had promised to write to Muthusawmy when he required him. The first of April now happened to come round; and the late Sir T. Madava Rao who was then a clerk in the Accountant-General's office and Dewan Bahadur Raghunatha Rao who was for some time Dewan of Indore conjointly manufactured a letter purporting to come from Sir Henry Montgomery and requiring

Muthusawmy to call at his house in Adyar. The young man was naturally highly elated, and having donned his best attire, gleefully set out for Sir Henry's house, accompanied by the two practical jokers. At the corner of the Mylapore tank, however, these latter had to part company from Muthusawmy; but they were unwilling to carry the joke any further and so asked him to carefully read the letter which he was carrying in his pocket. This he did, but failed to discover anything amiss and it was only when they raised a fold in a corner of the letter, and displayed the words "You are an April Fool," that the future Judge realised that his fond hopes of immediate employment had been ruthlessly dashed to the ground. However, in a few days, a genuine letter from Sir H. Montgomery arrived and Muthusawmy was employed in the Collectorate of Tanjore.

This office he held till 1st March 1856, when Sir Alexander Arbuthnot, then Director of Public Instruction, took him into his own Department as a Deputy Inspector of Schools on a salary of Rupees 150; and here he earned a name by his powers of organisation. But he was soon compelled to sever his connection with the Educational Department. Just at this time the Madras Government instituted an examination known as the "Pleader's Test" and those who passed it, it was notified would be allowed to practise in the Sudder as well as the Mofussil courts of the Presidency. In February 1856 the first examination was held. Kumbakonam was one of the examination centres, and Mr. J. T. Beauchamp, the Civil Judge, as he was then known, was appointed to conduct the examination at that station. Several candidates appeared; but only three succeeded, Muthusawmy Aiyar and Dewan Bahadur Raghunatha Rao coming off first and second respectively. One portion of the test consisted in writing a judgment in a case taken from the records of the Court, all the necessary information being read out to the candidates. The case placed before the Examinees at Kumbakonam related to an agreement which had been made between two heirs, as to how the property should be divided between them. The parties subsequently quarrelled and came to Court. The question at issue was whether any agreement between the parties, which was contrary to the terms of Hindu Law was binding upon them. The Appellate Court having reversed the decision of the Original Court in this case, there was some scope for the display of legal ingenuity. As the Sheristadar of the Civil Court was reading out the facts of the case to the candidates there was an altercation between him and Muthusawmy Aiyer, who could not quite follow the Sheristadar. Mr. Beauchamp's attention was attracted by the dispute; and on learning that the Sheristadar was reading too quickly, the Judge decided in order to secure fair treatment for the candidates, to consider himself an examinee and also take down the facts of the case and write a judgment thereon. Muthusawmy Aiyer's judgment tallied in every respect with Mr. Beauchamp's *viz.*, that the agreement, even if contrary to Hindu Law would be binding on the parties.

Mr. Beauchamp, soon after, appointed Muthusawmy Aiyar as District Munsiff of Tranquebar. Sir Alexander Arbuthnot objected to the transfer, but Mr. Holloway having been equally anxious to have him in the Judicial Department, prevailed upon the former. Muthusawmy Aiyar's work as a Munsiff was highly spoken of in the District. On one occasion Mr. Beauchamp wishing to inspect the office, resolved to take the Munsiff by surprise. He went to Tranquebar without previous announcement; but Muthusawmy Aiyar, hearing of his arrival saw him at his lodgings and, contrary to the general dread among Munsiffs in those days when District Judges go to their Courts for inspection, requested the Judge to grant him the favour of a searching inspection of his office, and of sitting with him on the Bench to witness how he conducted cases. The Judge attended the Court and was highly delighted with the excellent manner in which the Munsiff conducted cases and kept the registers in the office. The Judge returned to Tanjore and expressed it as his opinion that "Muthusawmy was one of those who was fitted to sit with him on the same Bench."

Muthusawmy Aiyar was again compelled to give up the department in which he served. Just about this time an Inam Commission was appointed with the object, as Sir Charles Trevelyan said, "of quieting the possession and giving the Inamdars proprietary titles." A number of educated youths was asked to join the Commission and one of them was Muthasawmy Aiyar. He was appointed Deputy Collector of Tanjore on the 2nd July 1859, and was placed in charge of two Taluqs. This duty he discharged with marked ability. In July 1862, he was made Deputy Collector and Magistrate, first of Arcot and then of Tanjore. As Deputy Collector and Magistrate, he displayed not only considerable aptitude for revenue work, but also a thorough knowledge of the criminal law of the country. Once a rich Sowcar was charged with the offence of cheating, and Mr. Morris the Collector, referred the case to Muthusawmy Aiyar for proper inquiry. Mr. J. B. Norton appeared before him to conduct the case, and after a prolonged trial for about fifteen days, the Magistrate committed the Sowcar to the Sessions. Mr. Norton was so much struck with Muthusawmy Aiyar's abilities, that on his return to Madras he told his friends, Mr. Holloway and Sir Aloxandcr Arbuthnot, that "much judicial talent of a very high order was wasted in the Revenue Department."

Jnst at this time there was wanted at the Mangalore Court a Judicial officer well acquainted with Procedure and Muthusawmy Aiyar was appointed Sub-Judge of South Canara, on the 9th July 1865. In July 1868 he was appointed a Magistrate of Police at Madras, and confirmed in that appointment on the death of the late Mr. Maskell. While employed in this capacity, Mr. Holloway, advised him as to the best means of acquiring a sound grasp of the principles of Law, and, in conformity with that eminent Judge's directions, Muthusawmy Aiyar carefully worked up the principles of Jurisprudence, and even learnt sufficient German in order to enable him to study the "tough Teutonic Treatises" on this subject. After he had thoroughly mastered Jurisprudence, Mr. Holloway made him analyse every judgment of the High Court and of the Privy Council and submit it to the rigid test of the principles of Jurisprudence. Mr. Holloway himself carefully revised all that Muthusawmy Aiyar wrote and not infrequently judgments thus analysed were found to be not exactly in conformity with the strict principles of Jurisprudence. To this training Muthusawmy Aiyer in later life ascribed the remarkable power which he possessed of accurately analysing cases.

One important feature of Muthusawmy Aiyar's character as a Judge was his stern devotion to duty and the conscientious discharge of his work without fear or favour. As an instance we may mention that when he was Police Magistrate, a native who had been thrashed by a European Judge of the High Court for alleged trespass into the latter's premises applied for a summons against that official for assault. Muthusawmy Aiyar immediately granted a summons without resorting to the temporising process of issuing a notice to show cause and though his senior on the bench suggested to him not to insist on the appearance of the High

Court Judge at the trial, Muthusawmy Aiyar would not yield and caused the High Court Judge to appear before him and fined him Rs. 3.

While employed as a Magistrate he studied for the B. L. Examination and passed it in the First Class. Referring to his success, Mr. John Bruce Norton said in one of his annual speeches at Pachaiyappa's College :—"Let me mention our excellent fellow-townsman and Magistrate, Muthusawmy Aiyer, who has never relinquished his studies; and at his age, and while occupying a seat on the Bench, he has had the moral courage to present himself for examination for the B. L. Degree. Rumour speaks of his having done excellently well; and indeed, I hear that he has obtained a First Class. If he is not at the head of the list, he has only been beaten by a very few marks by a younger competitor, who, it must be remembered, has had the advantage of being able to devote his entire time to his studies, while Muthusawmy has had all his magisterial duties to perform, and has only been able to devote his leisure to fitting himself for his examination. There have been first-class men in the B. L. Degree before; but then the standard was two-thirds of the whole number of marks; now it has been raised to three-fourths."

The result of the admirable work he did as a Magistrate was that he was elevated to the Small Cause Court as a Judge. So great was the satisfaction he gave to the Madras Government as a Small Cause Court Judge that Lord Hobart, the then Governor, appointed him District Judge of Cuddapah; but objection was taken to the appointment in certain quarters, and he had to give it up.

In January 1877, the Madras Government honoured him with an invitation to be present at the Imperial Assemblage at Delhi, and he received on that occasion a commemoration medal from the Viceroy. In 1878, he was admitted to the Companionship of the Order of the Indian Empire in recognition of his valuable services. In investing him with the Insignia of the Order, the Duke of Buckingham and Chandos, the then Governor said: "Muthusamy Aiyar,—The pleasing duty has fallen to me to deliver to you the Insignia of the Order of the Indian Empire in accordance with the grant which has just been read. You belong to a branch of the service, the judicial branch, of the highest importance to the well-being of the Empire. There is no branch of the service on whose efficiency, on whose integrity, and on whose ability and calm judgment, the liberty of the subject so entirely depends as upon the judicature. I have great satisfaction in observing that you who have distinguished yourself in this branch have been called forward to occupy a high and prominent place among the Judges of the land, and it is with great pleasure that it falls to me to announce to you that it has been Her Majesty's pleasure to select you for this favour, a favour which, I trust, you may long enjoy."

In the same year, Muthusawmy Aiyar was raised to the High Court bench and the Duke referred to his appointment in the following terms in one of his public speeches :—"In nominating the Hon'ble Sashia Sastri to the Council of the Viceroy, in placing the Hon'ble Mr. Justice Muthusawmy Aiyer on the Bench of our own High Court . . . , I know that I have advanced them to no honor which was not well deserved or to a post which would not be well filled. Such are the men of whom one shall hereafter need many more—keep them in your minds as studies for your emulation." When Muthusawmy Aiyar was elevated to the High Court Bench, he owned to a feeling of considerable diffidence as to his ability to cope with the work. It was the first time that a Native of India had been elevated to such an exalted position, and Muthusawmy Aiyer confessed to experiencing feelings of considerable trepidation when he tried his first case; and to his dismay one of the first cases which were put up before him was a breach of promise trial. As a Hindu, he was a complete stranger to European manners and customs—and he feared that his unfamiliarity with European life would lead him to some egregious blunders. He however, carefully studied the evidence and wrote and re-wrote his judgment several times before delivering it. With positive fear and trembling he read his judgment out in open Court, and to his intense relief and satisfaction it met with great commendation from the members of the Bar.

Other hard-won successes followed and in the process of a short time he was on all sides recognised to be one of the ablest Judges who adorned the High Court Bench. His calm, dispassionate behaviour on the Bench, his industrious and systematic habits, his wonderful memory, his powerful grasp of the minutest details in cases that were posted for hearing before him, and above all, his laborious discrimination of truth from falsehood, be the mass of evidence however great—all these marked him out as a model Judge. His legal conception of things presented to him was, like Lord Eldon's very accurate. His decisions are acknowledged to be fit to take rank with those of the best English Judges. It is bare truth to say that the most intricate cases were posted particularly before him in the High Court for disposal. He firmly believed that the duty of a Judge was sacred and he described it thus in his Convocation Address to the graduates of the Madras University. "The Court of Justice is a sacred temple, the Judges presiding over it are, though men, the humble instruments in the interests of truth, and those who enter this holy edifice with unholy thoughts or desecrate it with unworthy actions, are traitors to their God and country. Those of you who may rise to the Bench should recollect that the power you may be called upon to exercise in the name of your sovereign is, according to another of your ancestors, a power divine."

The European Judges with whom he sat, one and all regarded him as a great authority upon all principles of law. Dissents from his opinion were rare and his judgments, though often very long, were always exhaustive. They are valuable contributions to Indian legal literature. In the general introduction to his "Anglo-Indian Codes," Mr. Whitley Stokes says :—"My principal source of help has been the decisions of the High Court Judges published in the Indian Reports from 1862 to 1886 inclusive—decisions which not only throw light on the ideas and customs of the people of India, but are, as a rule, (if I may say so without impertinence) admirable for their logicality and learning. Of these Judgments, none can be read with more pleasure and few with more profit than those of the Hindu Muthusawmy Aiyar and the Mahomedan Sayyed Mahmood. For the subtle races that produce such lawyers no legal doctrine can be too refined, no legal machinery can be too elaborate." Muthusawmy Aiyar adorned the Bench for over fifteen years eliciting golden opinions from every one he came in contact with, and he attained the highest position open to a native of India in the Judicial Department in the country, when he acted as Chief Justice for three months in 1893. Soon afterwards he was made a K.C.I.E. and on that occasion, he was congratulated universally by natives as well as Europeans. The heavy and taxing duties of an Indian Judge brought to a speedy termination his brilliant career. Towards the beginning of the year 1895, he suddenly took ill and passed away to the regret of all his countrymen.

As a Judge he found little leisure to attend to other duties but he always took very great interest in matters connected with the Madras University. He was made a Fellow of the University in the year 1872 and became a member of the Faculty of Arts in 1877. He was for many years an Examiner in the B.L. and M.L. Examinations; and in all discussions on educational questions coming up before the Senate he took an active part. In connection with the University, he instituted a prize in the name of Mr. Carmichael who was a member of the Madras Council. He was the first native gentleman who was called upon to address the graduates on the Convocation day, and he discharged that duty with great credit and success. Sir T. Muthuswamy Aiyar was not accustomed to make public speeches, but the written addresses he delivered were characterised by sober suggestions clothed in simple but choice words.

His opinions of some of his contemporary public men are interesting. Of Mr. Powell, to whose tuition he owed his greatness, he always spoke in terms of reverence and affection. According to him, he was the best friend the natives have ever had in this Presidency. In no educational speech of his, Sir. T. Muthusawmy failed to pay a tribute of gratitude to his "revered master." Of Rai Bahadur T. Gopal Row, he used to say: "He is the only person whom I have throughout my life admired." Of Mr. Ranga Charlu of Mysore, he said that he was "really a great man, possessing a colossal intellect, while his powers of organisation were very astonishing." The late Professor Runganada Mudelliar was also held in high esteem by him, and at the meeting held to mourn his loss, Sir T. Muthusawmy Aiyar referred to him thus: "The very first conversation we had, inspired me with a feeling of high esteem and regard for him—an esteem and regard, which, I may tell you every day of my subsequent acquaintance only tended to enhance, until they ripened into a strong feeling of personal attachment."

It is often remarked that Sir T. Muthusawmy Aiyar did little to further the cause of Social Reform in this country. But he had not on that account failed to recognise the necessity for improving Hindu society in certain respects. He believed that the mending of Hindu Society must be brought about slowly and gradually. His views were broad, but in action he was cautious. His public addresses bear testimony to this fact. Speaking of the status of Hindu women, he said "No one who considers the social status of Hindu women can fail to come to the conclusion that it is open to considerable amendment." On female education, his opinion was "all of you should endeavour to secure the benefit of teaching to such young women as may come under your protection and guardianship, and I have no doubt that the prejudice against it will wear away in the same manner in which it has worn away in relation to girls receiving any education at all."

He was not opposed to foreign travel. "I will advise those of you who can afford to pay a visit to Europe," said he, "to do so and add to your knowledge the benefit of that social education which residence in civilised countries for a time, with a view to self-improvement, is likely to ensure." Here is his declaration on infant marriage :—"There is no foundation for the belief that a marriage contracted after maturity is illegal though in practice the supposed sin of the father was often visited by society upon the daughter." His opinion on re-marriage of widows was more pronounced :—"Although a woman could marry but once, a man is entitled to marry as often as he likes even when he has several wives living. This inequality between man and woman with respect to the rights and obligations of marriage, is aggravated by the incidents of the family system. . . . In these circumstances, it is no matter for surprise that friends of progress should characterise the social system and the law on which it rests as cruel to women. Considering it in relation to the requirements of morality, I must say that re-marriage is as necessary in the case of young widows whose marriages have been consummated as in the case of virgin widows."

It has been frequently asserted that, he did not take advantage of the opportunities he had as a Judge to facilitate social reform. His opinion was : "It must be remembered that the Hindu Law which the Courts are bound to administer is the law as received by the Hindu community and not as it stood either in the Vedic or Smrithic period of their history, and that no other conception of Hindu Law to be administered by the Court is either judicial or rational." Holding this view, he was still for progress in society, and on the broad issue of legislative interference he said: "It seems to me that the orthodox party overlooks the fact that a ruling power which recognises neutrality as the key-stone of all legislative and administrative action, and which has to deal with forms of marriage as numerous as there are races who owe allegiance to it, should interpose no obstacle in the path of progress, but that it should recognise the forms of marriage which the party in favour of reform may introduce from time to time. On the other hand, the party in favour of progress forgets that no statesman should be invited to commit himself to a course of legislative action which would invalidate marriages that are performed in accordance with national custom, and which would thereby involve in it an irritating interference with the most important domestic event of the majority of Her Majesty's Hindu subjects." Perhaps, it was a close knowledge of the opinions of Sir T. Muthusawmy Aiyar on social matters that made Dr. Duncan say in his Convocation address, (1891): "Are you afraid lest the good cause should make shipwreck at the outset by the intemperate advocacy of those whose zeal is apt to carry them beyond the bounds of prudence and legality? This difficulty can surely be met and overcome by a society which possesses men with the judicial acumen and calmness of the Hon'ble Mr. Justice Muthusawmy Aiyar."

On religion, Sir T. Muthusawmy Aiyar held a decided opinion. He acted on the belief that religion is indispensable to man. Believing in the existence of a Supreme Being from whom all good emanates, he did not fail to adopt even the conventional form of expressing his gratitude to his Maker and to offer solemn prayers to Him every day. The every day duty of a Brahmin of performing *pooja,* he practised. With him, it was a warm and vigorous dictate of the heart, and he did it, not as a policy but on principle and conviction. He had very great respect for those who were learned in the Vedas and it is worth mentioning that he supported a *Patasala* for the revival of the Shastras and other sacred writings. He was scrupulous in observing the several rites and ceremonies ordained by the Hindu religion and was an ardent well-wisher of its revival in its true, pure form.

We have referred to the studious habits of Sir T. Muthusawmy Aiyar, and we shall now mention a few of his favourite books. Shakespeare was one of his very favourite authors, and he and Rai Bahadur T. Gopal Row whenever they met, used to read a play together, and often dispute the meanings of particular passages. Sometimes a very hot debate would ensue, but these little debates were always of a very instructive kind.

Milton he had no particular liking for. Among prose writers of modern times he often read Carlyle and always Oliver Goldsmith, the latter being his chief favourite. He had read the "Vicar of Wakefield" not less than fifty times. He used to say that Gibbon was the study of the late Raja Sir Madava Row, Addison, of Mr. Seshiah Sastri and Shelley and Shakespeare of Rai Bahadur T. Gopal Row. His wonderful memory was almost the key to his enviable success in life. In the study of his books and in the hearing of cases, his memory helped him a great deal. He had only to read three times anything he wished to remember. We have also heard it often said that after hearing a case he could write out the judgment even after an interval of six months. In the schooldays of Sir T. Muthusawmy Aiyar, students cultivated memory as a regular art. Each student selected a book aud got it by heart so that he might re-write the whole without the help of the book.

Sir T. Muthusawmy Aiyar was from his boyhood industrious, patient, and well-behaved. Petted by every one of his friends and masters he was naturally a little haughty in his schooldays, but the harness of office, the acquisition of more knowledge and the experience of age made him revere and obey his superiors, love and respect his equals and encourage and advise the young.

Modesty and obedience were the essentials of his success in life. To whom else could Col. Hughes-

Hallett have referred when he addressed the Madras graduates of 1888 thus: "You have in this town, among your own countrymen, a living proof that the greatest abilities and the greatest industry may go hand-in-hand with extreme modesty, and may yet win not only the highest personal esteem but also the highest official rewards?" It was also his force of character that lifted him high in the eyes of his superiors.

He had a liking for natural objects and the Fine Arts. He had a passionate love for music as indicated in his excellent public address in Pachaiyappa's Hall during Lord Reay's visit to Madras. Sir M. E. Grant Duff referred to it in these words:—"I had great cause during the last few years to admire my honorable friend in many capacities, but I am not aware that he was also an authority upon that art which begins where all others end, which, when sculpture, painting and poetry respectively have had their say, takes up our thoughts, and carries them so far, I suppose, as it is permitted for them to be carried, while here in this state of existence." The name of Sir T. Muthusawmy Aiyar the first Native Jurist in the Madras Presidency is intended to be perpetuated by the erection of his marble statue in the Law Courts in Madras.

RAI BAHADUR T. GOPAL ROW, B.A.

Rai Bahadur Tandalam Gopal Row was born in the year 1832 in Ganapati Agraharam, a village on the banks of the Cauvery, near Kumbhakonam. He was a member of a Mahratta family of Western India which migrated to Tanjore with the early Mahratta Princes. His grandfather Tandalam Jeevanna *alias* Ramachandra Pundit was employed first under the Tanjore Raja and subsequently as a Tahsildar in the British service. His son Bava Pundit *alias* Raghava Punt, the father of Gopal Row, was also employed under the Rajah of Tanjore, the well-known Serfoji, in his Revenue Cutcherry. He had five sons and the youngest of them was Gopal Row. After a stay of about three years at Ganapati Agraharam, the place of Gopal Row's birth, where Bava Pundit was employed, he removed to Tiruvadi. From Tiruvadi, the family migrated to Travancore on the invitation of Dewan Runga Row, the father of Raja Sir T. Madava Row; and two of Bava Pundit's sons were at once taken into the Travancore service. Bava Pundit died while in Travancore and his family, including Gopal Row, returned to Tanjore.

Gopal Row had received from his father a good education in Marathi and Sanscrit, along with his four brothers; and for his elementary education in English he was indebted to one "English" Devaji Row. The complete mastery he subsequently acquired over the English language, was due entirely to his own exertions. Four years before his death, he said "I owe my education to no School or College. At fifteen, I was left to educate myself, as best I could, with just such a smattering of English as private tuition in the Mofussil could give thirty-five years ago; and whatever knowledge of Western literature or science I have acquired, has been acquired by unaided study—unaided in the most absolute sense. Books have been my only teachers."

In his seventeenth year, he entered public service as a clerk in the office of the Collector of Tanjore and in the space of two years, he was promoted to the responsible position of Manager of the Department of Public Works. He held this appointment for three years and during this period he rendered valuable service to Government by resolutely setting his face against all corruption. Mr. Holloway, who was then Assistant Collector at Tanjore and who afterwards became one of the Judges of the High Court, always spoke in high terms of Gopal Row's "very able and faithful services;" and none better appreciated the worth of Gopal Row in after years than Mr. Holloway.

In 1854, Gopal Row entered the Educational Department as First Assistant in the

Provincial School at Kumbakonam. In 1857, the Madras University was established and Gopal Row succeeded in passing the Matriculation Examination in that very year. In 1859, he appeared for the B. A. Examination and came off first, being placed alone in the first-class. This success of Gopal Row was remarkable considering that at the time, he was a schoolmaster with six hours of school work on an average. Mr. Forbes, then a member of the Governor-General's Legislative Council, wrote to him from Calcutta as follows :—" Although I have not heard from you to tell me, I cannot doubt that you are the man who has taken his B. A. degree at the University lately, and I am unwilling that you should suppose that I am not sufficiently interested in you to write and offer you my congratulations. I think that your success is very highly creditable to your talents and your industry, and I hope that you will let it stimulate you to further exertion." Mr. Holloway wrote to him thus :—"My letters are not many but I could not resist my desire of telling you, on this interesting occasion, how sincerely I rejoice in your present success and desire your future happiness and prosperity."

The rest of Gopal Row's life was spent in the Educational Department and during the greater portion of it, he was connected with the Kumbakonam College. The reputation of this College was chiefly due to two men, Mr. Porter and Rai Bahadur Gopal Row. The teaching of Mathematics and English in this institution chiefly devolved on Gopal Row: and

Mr. E. B. Powell, the pioneer of higher education in Southern India spoke of Gopal Row's work as "nowhere surpassed." During the years 1870, 1871 and 1872, Gopal Row acted as an Inspector of Schools and that was the very first instance of a native being appointed to such a responsible post in the Educational Department. During this period he performed his duties in a careful and conscientious manner and did his best to render sounder the instruction given in the schools under his charge. The Madras Government observed that the experiment of employing a native as an Inspector of Schools had been tried and proved a decided success. In recognition of his singular ability, Gopal Row was nominated a Fellow of the Madras University.

From 1872 to 1874, he was in sole charge of the Kumbakonum College. The results achieved during these years by the College were even more brilliant than those obtained during Mr. Porter's time, and the then Director of Public Instruction in his report to Government, remarked :—"Mr. Gopal Row has most satisfactorily established his fitness to preside over the second College in the Presidency, should a vacancy occur in the Principalship." But he was never confirmed as Principal of the College. In 1878 he was admitted into the graded service as Professor of History and Political Economy in the Presidency College. The action of Government in long withholding from such an excellent educationist a place in the graded service gave much pain to the native community. The Government of India, however, in recognition of his educational service, conferred on him the title of "Rai Bahadur" as a personal distinction.

The last years of Gopal Row were spent in the Presidency College as Professor of History. In 1883, he had a severe attack of fever due to over-exertion of his mental faculties. Since then he never recovered his full strength. For two years more he continued to work as Professor but finding that his health was failing, he took furlough for six months and proceeded to Kumbakonam for rest. But he never resumed his duties again. He was taken back to Madras in a state of serious illness and he passed away quietly on the 11th May 1886.

The news of his death was received with universal regret. The Presidency College Council placed on record "their appreciation of his long public services and of his personal character." Dr. D. Duncan, the Director of Public Instruction in Madras, in intimating to Government the death of Rai Bahadur Gopal Row, referred in the following terms to his services as an Educationist:—"Having entered the department in October 1854, he (Gopal Row) had completed a service of over thirty-seven years. During this long period he rendered most valuable service to Government and the public. A good Mathematician, Mr. Gopal Row was nevertheless better known as an English scholar. As a teacher of the English language and literature he stood in the first rank, even when compared with the best European teachers of that subject. Having had the good fortune to be intimately associated with him in the Presidency College and the University during recent years, I am in a position to estimate the greatness of the loss which the cause of education has sustained by his death." "I have" wrote the same gentleman to Gopal Row's eldest son on the 26th May 1886: "I have known for many years and admired him for his pre-eminent intellect and moral qualities. Latterly it has been my privilege to be closely associated with him in the Presidency College, and when I look back upon our intercourse during these years, I cannot remember a single incident having occurred to break the harmony of our friendship. The members of the Department of which he was such an ornament sympathise deeply with you in your affliction, and feel that your loss is also theirs."

Equally flattering was the testimony of other men who had known Gopal Row intimately. "None of the many friends of your late lamented father" wrote Rai Bahadur P. Runganada Mudaliar to Gopal Row's son "can feel deeper sorrow than I do, or appreciate more keenly the loss that the Native community of Southern India has suffered by his untimely death." Sir T. Muthusawmy Iyer said that among his educated countrymen, he hardly knew one who had a stronger claim to public recognition in Tanjore than his much lamented friend, Gopal Row, or who had rendered more useful service to the cause of liberal education. He added, "I first met him in 1854, and I have ever since uniformly respected and admired him. To a superior mind which he richly cultivated for upwards of thirty years, and to literary attainments of a very high order which he owed less to Colleges than to self-teaching and well-directed industry, he united a rare purity of character and devotion to duty. He struck me in many ways as being what a man of high education and culture should be. His career in Kumbakonum, first as Mr. Porter's Assistant, and afterwards as his successor, is well known to you. It is part of the history of liberal English education in Tanjore, and he has nobly earned for himself a conspicuous position in that history. I have reason to think that if it had pleased Providence to spare him to us for a few years longer he would have done something in retirement to improve our literature. I feel that in his premature death the people of Tanjore have lost one of their brightest ornaments; the educated classes a rare model of high culture and worth in private and public life; and his pupils, an Educationist who often reminded one of Messrs. Powell and Porter."

The Hon'ble and Rev. Dr. Miller, the well-known Principal of the Madras Christian College delivered himself thus in the *Christian College Magazine*:—"We wish only to join with others in expressing deep regret at the too early removal from our midst of one who held most deservedly so high a place in the esteem of the community at large, and of those members of it in particular who watch with interest the process by which the India that is to be is emerging from the India that has been. That is no disparagement to many well-known names when we say that few of the educated sons of Southern India held so high a place in the regard of Natives and Europeans equally, and that fewer still have done so much to mould the generations that are to come, as he who has now passed away. Engrossed in the work he had to do, unobtrusive and unambitious, Mr. Gopala Row has yet had an influence both healthier and more enduring than that of many whose names have been far more widely sounded. As an Examiner and Fellow of the University, as an Inspector of Schools, most of all as a Teacher, he set himself to do thoroughly, to do as well as it admitted of being done—the work which his hands had found. For the rewards which sometime follow, and which ought to follow successful work, he cared comparatively little. To him the question of fulfilling duty was always the paramount one; and in deciding on the way of fulfilling it he taught for himself and judged for himself. He was little swayed by popular prejudice or party cries. When convinced that the course he had chosen was the right one, it mattered little to him whether popularity or unpopularity was its immediate outcome to himself. Few things are more urgently required at present than that in these respects—not to speak of others—his example should be followed by the educated men of Southern India.

"Some among those to whom Mr. Gopal Row's memory is dear will be disposed, unless we are mistaken, to regret that talents so great and a character so high never raised the possessor to a loftier position in the world and never gained him more wide-spread fame. In this regret we can hardly share. It is the quiet flowing stream that does most to fertilize the valley with its waters. If even a few of the many hundreds whom he helped to train exhibit in coming years that earnestness in duty, that superiority to petty aims, that determination to have every question thought out and decided on its proper grounds which characterised their departed teacher, his life will have been more truly useful, and deserving therefore of higher honour, than the lives of many whose names have been bruited abroad more widely. We are glad to learn that steps are being taken to perpetuate the memory of Mr. Gopala Row in the town where most of his active life was spent. This is well; but a still better and more lasting monument will be erected in his honour if those whom he taught and trained will guide their own lives by the moral principles which animated his, and by so doing bring those principles to bear with living power on those whom they will influence in turn."

To these highly flattering notices of Rai Bahadur Gopal Row's life we have the pleasure to add the testimony of Mr. Porter. In a private letter to one of his friends he wrote :—"The news of Mr. Gopal Row's death, which reached me about a fortnight ago, was a great surprise and sorrow to me. I had written to him two months before, and my letter was acknowledged by his son, who said his father was not very well, but I thought nothing of it, and was always expecting to hear from him his opinion of a book which I had sent him, when the Maharajah of Mysore mentioned in a letter that Gopal Row was dangerously ill. His life has been a most useful one: and as regards myself, I am able to look back on a friendship with him of twenty years, never once disturbed by a single unpleasant word or act."

It is as a teacher that Gopal Row lives in the memory of the people of Southern India and we cannot give a better idea of him as a teacher, than by quoting the words of one of his successful pupils, who in the course of a speech delivered in the Porter Town Hall, Kumbaconum, gave a most faithful picture of the recollections he had of Gopal Row :—"As a teacher, he was a thorough-going man. Everything that he did and said was characterised by genuineness. There was no Brummagem at all. In addition to teaching the text, he introduced into his teaching a great deal of collateral matter, the moral influence of which cannot be forgotten. Thrilling quotations, interesting anecdotes, spirited narratives; and great sayings of great men came in rapid succession; at one moment he would speak about the world's greatest intellect, namely, Aristotle, at another of Shelley, and then again about the Poet-philosopher, Wordsworth; at one time he would speak about the genius of Pascal, at another of the Greek and Roman heroes. He used to speak occasionally also about the great heroes of the Madras University, of Pœzold, and Sanjiva Row, of Subramania Aiyar and Ranganadam, and bid his pupils emulate and imitate them. He tried every means for elevating us:—

> 'As a bird each fond endearment tries.
> To tempt its new-fledged offspring to the skies,
> He tried each art, reproved each dull delay,
> Allured to brighter worlds and led the way.' "

In his younger days Gopal Row seems to have taken delight in drawing; and he acquired from his father a taste for Marathi literature which he kept up to the last. His early compositions in Marathi verse have been lost; but his metrical translation of Goldsmith's "Hermit," which he composed a few months before his death, is still extant, and is appreciated for the chasteness of its style and the faithful delineation of the beauties of the original. He delighted the family circle by the recital of numerous Sanskrit and Marathi verses, which he easily fixed in his strong memory and delivered with the same peculiar charm, with which in later years, he entertained his pupils, by reciting well-known passages from his favourite English poets. He had a good taste for Music and appreciated the finest touches of it, with an amount of discrimination rarely to be met with.

It was, indeed, a treat to listen to him whenever he spoke of his favourite English poets and more especially of Shelley, his greatest favourite. Though he did not excel as a public speaker, yet in private conversation he was most impressive and instructive. As Mr. Porter has well expressed in one of his letters to a friend, "Gopal Row's life was spent in educating his fellow-citizens quite as much by his conversation as by his direct teaching." His choice, chaste English, expressed in clear ringing tones often rose into fervid eloquence and kept his hearers in wrapt attention. He was always possessed of a clear head. Everything he said was deeply thought out and logically expressed. He was ever willing to learn from all with whom he came in contact, and never obtruded his views on others. To the end of his life he remained a student.

Gopal Row's intellectual attainments were certainly of no mean order. What made his very name inspire the deepest admiration and reverence was the moral grandeur of his character. Genius may inspire awe and men may look upon geniuses with the same feelings as they view a work of fine art full of sublimity, but intellectual greatness must be combined with moral goodness in order that men may be *influenced*. The very name "Gopal Rao" has in Kumbaconum and among his pupils and friends become synonymous with all that is just, upright and honest. His deep sense of right and duty made him at times intolerant of the frailties of others. He appeared sometimes hard and unsympathetic, and men of suspicious character trembled to appear before him. But as a rule his generosity and cheerfulness of temper drew always round him a band of enthusiastic admirers who looked up to him as their guide, philosopher, and friend.

Gopal Row was not a Social Reformer. Nevertheless, his views on Social Reform are worth quoting. The reforms which seemed to him most urgent were "(1) female education; (2) the abolition of early marriage; (3) the abolition of enforced widowhood; (4) the abolition of those distinctions without the slightest warrant from the Shastras which divide and keep asunder members of the same caste." Early marriage, he considered unquestionably to be the most crying of our social evils. "It is the bane and curse of Hindu Society. It is visibly deteriorating, and most visibly among that class of Hindus among whom it is most prevalent, *viz.*, the Brahmins. It is very rarely that one sees men and women of that class as tall and strong as their parents. Brahmins of the present day have little stamina: few of them are capable of vigorous and sustained exertion, bodily or mental. A few years' study seems in many cases to do serious injury to their constitution. Too many of them die untimely. It requires no profound knowledge of physiology to be convinced that youths of sixteen and seventeen and girls of twelve or thirteen must be incapable of producing mature offspring. The husbandman takes care that his seed paddy is mature and that his soil is well manured and prepared before he sows; and it is strange that the acute and quick-witted Hindu of the present day is unable to see that the analogy applies to the human frame." Enforced widowhood, he thought was "unquestionably productive of much misery and sin; and the cruelty involved in society inflicting all this misery on so many of its members and drawing them into this sin, becomes more flagrant when it is remembered that early widowhood is, in a great many cases, the result of early marriages, for which the contracting parties are by no means responsible."

RAI BAHADUR P. RUNGANADA MUDALIAR, M.A.

Rai Bahadur Pundi Runganada Mudaliar was born in Madras in 1837. He belonged to a respectable family of Mudaliars. His father Pundi Subbaraya Mudaliar, who was fairly well-educated in English, was for some time Manager of the Irrigation Canal Company. He fully appreciated the advantages of English education and took good care to educate his son at home, as at an early period, Runganadam showed signs of remarkable intellectual energy. While Runganadam was quite a lad, his father was transferred to Avanashi as Head Accountant of the Madras Railway. He, however, did not remain in this place long. One night Subbaraya Mudaliar's little cottage home was attacked by dacoits. The father fearing the harm that may happen to his favourite son, hid him in a wooden loft which was suspended to the roof, and gave himself up with his little daughter to the tender mercies of the dacoits. Everything in the house was surrendered and yet the dacoits were not satisfied. " You have more hidden somewhere" they said "and if you do not give up all, you shall pay for it with your life." Then the father had to confess tremblingly that his little son was hidden above. The young lad was brought down and had to plead in turn for his own life. This incident made Subbaraya Mudaliar leave Avanashi the next day and he, with his family, settled in Madras once more.

Runganadam's home education was attended to carefully by his father. The instruction he received in English could not have been of a very high character, but there cannot be the slightest doubt that Runganadam's passionate love for Tamil literature must have been to a great extent due to the instruction that he received at home under the superintendence of his beloved father.

In 1860, when Runganadam was thirteen years of age, he was sent to Pachaiappa's High School. He was admitted into the Third Class, corresponding to the present Fourth Form, which was taught by one Parthasarathy Iyengar, who afterwards became a Vakil of the High Court. This school, which was under the management of Mr. Basil Lovery, one of the distinguished educationists of the Presidency, was even then very popular with the Hindu community. Runganadam's remarkable attainments came under the notice of the Principal who took a personal interest in every lad in the school to whatever class he belonged. In the third class, Runganadam held a scholarship of Rs. 60 per annum, and he did so well at the annual examination that he was promoted to the First Class (Matriculation) at the beginning of the following year.

Here, under the immediate tuition of Mr. Lovery, he achieved greater distinction than he had done in the lower class. He carried away a number of prizes and won also the special prize offered by Rajah Sir T. Madava Row, for proficiency in English and Mathematics. An incident relating to Runganadam's scholastic career may be of interest to our readers as showing the great confidence which the lad had in his own intellectual powers and also his boldness which was a marked characteristic of his, till the end of his life. He was asked once to write an essay on "Female Education" for which a special prize was offered. When the essays of the youthful competitors came to be valued, the Examiners found the best were those of Runganadam and one Coopuram Sastri. The essays were then shown to Messrs. J. B. Norton and J. D. Mayne; Mayne preferred Runganadam's, whereas Norton gave the palm to Coopuram's essay. The essays were thereupon sent to another literary Judge, Mr. Justice Holloway, who decided in favour of Runganadam. But somehow or other, the prize was given to the other student. The decision did not satisfy Runganadam and he made up his mind to fight the battle out to the bitter end. On the day of the anniversary of the school which was presided over by the then Governor, Lord

Harris, Runganadam rushed from his seat with the essay in hand with a view to get the final verdict from the Governor himself. His masters knew what the lad was about, and it was with considerable difficulty that they persuaded him that the matter would be looked into by the authorities concerned.

In 1862, Runganadam matriculated, as first in the Presidency and in the same year he joined the Presidency College, with a stipendiary scholarship from the Trustees of the Pachaiyappa's College. Runganadam's collegiate career was even more brilliant. When he joined the Presidency College, that institution had just then entered upon a new era of progress. With Mr. Edmund Thompson as Principal and Professor of English literature, the College had begun to turn out men of a very superior type. Men like Pæzold and Snell and Nevins were giants in themselves, but Runganadam had determined to break the record and he succeeded. He was an "Admirable Crichton" in his own way. In Mathematics, in English, in Philosophy and in Tamil, there was none Runganadam's superior, and Mr. Thompson and his fellow Professors watched with the greatest interest the unfolding of the powers of a real man of genius. His fame spread far and wide and men even outside his College, such as Mr. E. B. Powell, the Director of Public Instruction, the late Mr. Justice Holloway and others began to take a deep interest in the career of this distinguished student. Though

Runganadam made Mathematics his special study, he succeeded in acquiring a mastery over the English language which would have done credit to any English Professor. He entered fully into the genius of the English language and wrote and spoke it with the fluency and grace of the most cultured English gentlemen.

In 1862, Sir Rama Varma the late Maharajah of Travancore (then First Prince) handed over a sum of money to the Senate of the Madras University to found a gold medal worth Rs. 300 to be awarded to the Bachelor of Arts who might stand highest in the First Class in the Degree Examination. Neither in 1863 nor in 1864 was the medal awarded, as no Bachelor secured a place in the First Class. In February 1865, the medal was carried off by Runganadam. Referring to Runganadam's success in the B.A. Examination, Mr. John Bruce Norton said in his annual address at the Pachaiappa's Institution in 1865 :—" Among the passed candidates at the recent Matriculation Examination, out of fifty, ten were *alumni* of Pachaiappa's; no less a proportion than one-fifth: of eleven who succeeded in obtaining the Degree of B.A., four were young men whose education commenced at Pachaiappa's; and of these P. Runganada Mudaliar obtained the first place. He passed, I understand, a highly creditable examination. He has also carried off the prize instituted by that most enlightened Prince, His Highness Rama Varma, the First Prince of Travancore; and

I hear on excellent authority, that he is a young man of singular promise." The prizes and medals he won at College were many and Mr. Thompson was so pleased with his pupil's career that he had Runganadam appointed as Assistant Master in the Presidency College, immediately after his passing the B. A. Degree examination.

Runganadam, in his choice of a profession, was no doubt, influenced by his European friends who were mostly educationists, but at the same time he was himself not unaware of the opportunities of usefulness he would have by adopting this profession; and hence it is that, though on more than one occasion he had tempting offers in other departments, he chose to remain a teacher till the end of his life. But the Madras Government recognized his services tardily, though no opportunity was lost to extol his abilities and the distinguished services he had rendered Government in his varied capacities as an educational officer. Before he was confirmed as Professor of Mathematices in the Presidency College he had to act sixteen years as Professor in some capacity or other.

In 1872 Runganada Mudaliar was appointed Fellow of the Madras University, and since 1875, till his death he was elected every year a member of the Syndicate. He took an active part in the deliberations of the Senate of the Madras University, and there was no native whose opinions on University questions were more respected than those of Runganada Mudaliar. In the Syndicate also his influence was very great and he always used it not to further the interests of any particular individual or clique, but to advance those of all classes, irrespective of caste or creed. There was not a single important Educational Committee or Commission of which he was not a member and in all these Runganada Mudaliar's ready pen was brought into requisition, no resolution or report being considered perfect until it had received the finishing touch of Runganada Mudaliar. In 1890 he was appointed Tamil Translator to Government, and in 1892, solely through the influence of Sir Henry Stokes, he was appointed Sheriff of Madras.

Not only as an educational officer, but also as a public citizen, Runganada Mudaliar was most useful to his countrymen. In all matters needing the interpretation of the views of the native public he was consulted. He took an active part in the deliberations of the Madras Municipality of which he was a member. The speeches he made at the Municipal meetings are some of the best specimens of English "pure and undefiled." He was the life and soul of the "Cosmopolitan Club," and the popularity of this institution was a great deal due to the fascinating influence of his personality.

In 1890 he had the honour of delivering the Convocation address to the graduates of the Madras University. The address was not marked by any originality but by sound common sense and was couched in the most elegant language. It was well received by the European and native public.

Mr. H. J. S. Cotton, the author of *New India*, happened to read the address and wrote as follows to Runganada Mudaliar :—"As a complete stranger I must apologise for writing to you that I have just had the pleasure of reading your University address and cannot omit telling you how excellent it reads to me from first to last. If I may do so without impertinence, I would heartily congratulate you on it. I hope it may be widely read, not only in Madras, but all over India and in England also."

Runganadam was a real ornament to the Native community and very few of its members expected that they would be called upon so soon as on the 10th December 1893 to mourn his loss. But so it happened. Runganada Mudaliar breathed his last after a few days' illness which none suspected would prove fatal. He was ailing from fever, brought on by overwork. He was in harness till the very end and attended College even four days before his death. His loss was mourned by all classes of people, European and Native. The Presidency College Council while placing on record its sense of the great loss the College had sustained by his sudden and untimely death, admitted that "he had filled with marked distinction, not only the Chair of Mathematics, but also those of Logic and Moral Philosophy and History" and that "his death has deprived the College of one who has rendered it invaluable services in various capacities."

Dr. Duncan, the Director of Public Instruction, who was one of Runganada Mudaliar's oldest colleagues and friends in the Presidency College, said in the course of a letter to Runganada Mudaliar's eldest son, that to the last Runganada Mudaliar retained the highest place in his esteem. "Perhaps" he added, "Perhaps, no European now in Madras had such a long and unbroken friendship with your father as I had, or had more opportunity of knowing his sterling qualities of mind and heart. A brilliant scholar, a loyal citizen, wise and prudent in council, and courteous in manners, he endeared himself to all who had the privilege of knowing him. I see that steps are to be taken to honor his memory in some tangible form, and I am glad to see so. But after all, the best way to commemorate him is to follow the example he set to his fellow-countrymen and to all of us."

Dr. Miller bore testimony to the admirable work Runganada Mudaliar did as a member of the Education Commission and his words are well worthy of reproduction :—"I think I may say that of all the sons of our University with whom I have at any time come in contact— nay, I would say of all the sons of India with whom in a public way I have had to deal—there has not been a single one so markedly valuable in this particular way, as the friend whose loss we are mourning now. There are many men amongst us who hold strong views upon public questions, many men who are able to express their views impressively and eloquently, and many men who are able to play the very useful part of an advocate or pleader of one side of the question, but there are extremely few in any land, and very few indeed I fear in this land, who are qualified calmly and dispassionately when public questions come before them, to exercise the still higher function of a Judge. But amongst these was he whose loss we are mourning now. In that Commission to which I have ventured to refer, there were many difficult questions to be considered, many questions about which much had been said on every side, many questions that had aroused feelings; but he whose loss we are mourning was not swayed by any considerations of that kind. He displayed beyond almost any member of the body the calm, dispassionate, far-reaching and wide view of the Judge—the quality which is, above all things, most important and most valuable to him who would be the guide to the community at large. There were few differences between him and me, between him and most of his colleagues at the beginning of our discussions, and there were none of any importance at the end. For the wonderful unanimity that characterized the decisions arrived at by the Commission, composed though it was of the most varied and discordant elements, dealing with most difficult questions, we were most largely indebted to the calm judgment and the far-reaching grasp of Mr. Runganada Mudaliar. There were strong men on that Commission, Sir, few men stronger than one, whose loss all educated India was called to mourn only a brief period before Mr. Runganadam himself was taken away from us, Mr. Justice Telang of Bombay. There was that ornament of educated Indian Society, and there were others, too, whom I will not name, because they still are doing honoured and useful work for the benefit of this ancient land; but amongst them all there were but few, and perhaps not even one, who in a quiet and steady way did more useful and more lasting work than the friend who has been taken from us."

Runganada Mudaliar was a teacher: nevertheless, he was esteemed by Dr. Miller more as a fair and impartial judge of men and measures. To this intelligent appreciation of Runganada Mudalliar's abilities it is interesting to add what an eminent judge thought of the Professor. "Close acquaintance and friendship" said Sir T. Muthusawmy Aiyar in the course of his speech at the Runganadam memorial meeting in February 1894," "Close acquaintance and friendship soon convinced me that as a public man his merits were pre-eminent. His devotion to public duty, his services as a teacher and a professor, as an educationist and as a friend of progress, were invaluable. His industry and perseverance were remarkable, and he had a marvellous devotion first to duty and next to study. His application to study was so close that it often reminded me of what the younger Pliny once wrote in speaking of his uncle, the elder Pliny. 'It makes me' said the former, 'smile when people call me a student, for compared with him, I am a mere idler. I remember his rebuking me once for taking a walk, and saying you might have managed not to lose these hours.' "

It was not so much his industry as his intelligence that made Runganada Mudaliar the unique figure he was in enlightened Hindu society. His intellectual versatility was at once the admiration and the envy of his numerous friends. He was not only a capable man and a ripe scholar, but also a practical man. He combined the rarest culture with the highest intellectual gifts. It was indeed a treat to listen to his brilliant conversations. His style was racy, sinewy and idiomatic; and he would often entertain his friends with some striking expression of some favourite author or other. As a speaker he was by no means eloquent, but he spoke with ease, fluency and grace, clothing his thoughts in the choicest language. He was passionately fond of English literature and his favourite poet was Shakespeare. Among prose writers his favourites were Lecky, Leslie Stephen, John Morley and Ruskin. His knowledge of Tamil literature was profound and in this department he was a match for any Pundit. Nothing he so much revelled in as quoting passages from the Ramayana and expounding them to his friends. He always deplored the neglect of the study of vernacular languages by the present generation of students.

Runganada Mudaliar was every inch a gentleman. He possessed the polished manners and high breeding which are so difficult of attainment and so strictly personal when attained, He possessed a very tender and sympathetic heart. A large portion of his income was spent on charities and in helping poor and deserving students. But whatever he did, he did secretly without telling others. He was most generous in the appreciation of gifts and talents in others. Of men like Mr. Telang of Bombay and Sir T. Muthusawmy Iyer he spoke in the most enthusiastic terms. Of the latter, he said :—" He is out-and-out the best man that modern India has produced, so far as intellectual acumen is concerned."

Runganada Mudaliar has not left any original work behind, except a poem in Tamil entitled "Kachikalandakam," but this work did not enhance his reputation as a scholar. He did not identify himself with any movement having for its object social reform. A man of his influence and talents, if he had only possessed the necessary enthusiasm, would have been a great power for good. His views on Social Reform are contained in the following brief extract from his Convocation address :—" Never lose sight of the fact that you have to carry the masses with you, and that in consequence some of the social and religious changes that the educated few may be ripe for will have to be postponed ; and that true wisdom and philanthropy require that while you have your faces set in the right direction, and while you have the courage to declare your convictions, you walk warily and slowly so that your less favoured brethren may follow your lead at such pace as is good for them. Observe, I do not commend the practice, which is only too prevalent, of talking and acting in a manner entirely at variance with one's own thoughts and feelings. Such incongruity between the inner and the outer life is the very death of all that is pure and noble and self-denying. According to the best light in you, approve only of what you consider to be right, and so conduct yourself as to make it clear, that you neither justify nor excuse injurious customs and debasing superstitions. The Western ideas and sentiments that you have imbibed in the course of your education will and must urge you to advance, but as in human affairs, good and evil are inextricably blended together, and the desire to obtain a thing is no guarantee of fitness to use the thing desired wisely and well, I would solemnly entreat you to look before you leap, and to make sure by observation, by study, and by reflection that in your impatient unwillingness to bear the ills you have, you do not fly to greater ills you know not of."

G. LAKSHMINARASU CHETTY, C.S.I.

Gazulu Lakshminarasu Chetty was born in the year 1806 in Periamet, Madras. His father Sidhulu Chetty was an indigo merchant in fairly affluent circumstances. Indigence was, therefore, no impediment in the way of his obtaining a sound English education. But in those days, there were few schools in which natives of India could learn the English language. The missionaries who were the first to establish English schools had not then come out to India in large members. The education given in schools started by native enterprise was hardly worth the name, and it was to one of such schools that Lakshminarasu was sent for education. The three R's was all that Lakshminarasu was able to learn in the Native Association Society's School. His father intended him merely to look after the family trade and learn the art of selling goods to the best advantage and keeping accounts. But it is said that even during his boyhood, Lakshminarasu evinced a predisposition to that remarkable individuality and fearless independence which characterised his subsequent career. While yet a boy, he joined Debating Societies and took more than a passing interest in the political questions of the hour.

On leaving school, he was apprenticed to his father's shop, and, after he learned, what in mercantile parlance is called, the tricks of the trade, he was made an active member of the firm; and the business was carried on by father and son under the style of Sidhulu Chetty and Co. The firm chiefly dealt in Madras handkerchiefs and throve apace especially after the death of Sidhulu Chetty which event left Lakshminarasu Chetty in sole possession of the large concern. The States of America happened just about this time to be involved in internal feuds which resulted in the temporary and sudden cessation of their cotton trade. This opened up a wide scope for speculation in other countries, especially Egypt and India. Lakshminarasu Chetty took advantage of the propitious hour and entered largely upon speculation in cotton. The trade throve considerably and in an inappreciably short time, Lakshminarasu Chetty was able to amass a large fortune.

With considerable wealth at his command, Lakshminarasu Chetty grew rather indifferent to his business and gave himself up heart and soul, to the task of achieving the political emancipation of his countrymen. The Hindus at the time, not having had the benefit of English education, were entirely ignorant of the nature of the Government to which they were the subject. To the suffering and ignorant Hindus the executive authorities in Madras constituted the entire ruling body. They did not know that these were subject to the authoritative control of a Board in England and that they could make representations to the Board about their grievances. Lakshminarasu Chetty was one of the few exceptions. He started the Madras Native Association of which he became President, for the purpose of ventilating from time to time on perfectly constitutional lines the people's grievances. Wealthy merchants and respectable non-officials became members of the Association and did very useful work. Meetings were often held for considering the grievances of the people and memorials were despatched to England for their redress.

Lakshminarasu Chetty's first political fight was with the European missionaries. The missionaries who had come out to India with the ostensible object of disseminating the learning and the literature of the West, after a very short residence in this country, made their original object a secondary one and set about proselytizing. Few Hindus knew the English language and as a knowledge of it was a condition precedent to the securing of any situation in Government offices, they were driven to the necessity of sending their children to missionary institutions for education. The missionaries converted the indigent and the helpless among them notwithstanding their tender years. The few Englishmen who held positions of any degree of authority or influence in the Presidency espoused the cause of the missionaries. The Collector of Tinnevelly, one Mr. Thomas, openly co-operated with the missionaries in his district in their efforts to spread the Christian religion. Sir William Burton, a Judge of the Madras Sadr Court, made no secret of his sympathy with the cause of the missionaries and now and then delivered sermons from his seat on the bench to the Hindus. Mr. J. F. Thomas, the then Chief Secretary to Government and a close relation of Mr. E. B. Thomas, Collector of Tinnevelly, provided Hindu converts to Christianity with appointments under Government in preference to Hindus. The District Judge of Chingleput, Mr. Morehead, postponed the hearing of causes set down on a certain day's list and threw his court-house open to a preacher of the gospel. The Madras Government carried their partiality for the Christian religion to such an extent as to remove from the Sadr Court a Judge who refused to carry out their unjust dictates. The following passage from Mr. Lewin's reply to an address from the Hindu community depicts the Government of the day in their true colours :—

"Had the Government met with no resistance in their attempt to coerce the judges of the Sadr Court into measures fatal to impartial justice, it is probable the next attempt would have been an open and undisguised one to force Christianity upon the Hindus. Although the Marquis of

Tweeddale has disclaimed these views, experience has abundantly proved that there are parties connected with the Government who had the will and the means to carry them out. The conduct of the Government towards the Sadr Court forced the Judges to resist an order which no Judge who knew his duty could submit to; that resistance was foreseen and calculated upon by the advisers of the Government, and there can be no doubt it was the first step of a scheme which was devised for the removal of the second Judge who had been more than once obliged to inform the Government that he was prepared at all hazards to uphold the integrity of his Court and to prevent its being made an instrument of injustice."

The malpractices of the Missionaries and the open and undisguised manner in which they were encouraged by Government Officials incensed the Hindu community greatly and Lakshminarasu Chetty resolved to do all that lay in his power to check the violation of the pledges which the British Power had given the people of India not to interfere with their religious observances. Just then there was in existence a newspaper called the *Native Circulator* edited by one Narayanasamy Naidu. Lakshminarasu Chetty purchased the paper and the press, changed the name of the paper to that of the *Crescent* and secured the services of one Mr. Harley as Editor. Mr. Harley was previously serving in the Army and brought to the conduct of his journal his military spirit and an untractable disposition. He was a man of very strong convictions. The first issue of the *Crescent* was given to the world on the 2nd October 1844. The object of the paper was stated to be "the amelioration of the condition of the Hindus." The *Crescent* was intended to act as a corrective on the *Record*, the declared missionary organ. It set itself to condemn the malpractices of the missionaries and expose their vagaries. For a time the *Crescent* incurred some odium. But in spite of all difficulties it firmly maintained its ground. The Judges and executive officials smarted under its scathing criticism, and unable to meet it by facts or reasoning, secretly assisted the work of the missionaries while they appeared impartial in the eyes of the public. The Government denied to the *Crescent* the smallest privileges which they willingly accorded to other newspapers of the day. The Manager of the *Crescent* sent an advertisement to the Government office regarding itself for insertion in the *Fort St. George Gazette*. The advertisement was returned as inadmissible with the endorsement of the Chief Secretary to Government that it was "of a character not usually inserted."

Meanwhile, the Government officials, to place the wordly prospects of converts above all danger determined to use their powers of legislation for their good and to enact a law under the provisions of which Hindu youth may become converts, to Christianity without the slightest prejudice to their rights in the property owned by their family.

The Hindu community protested against the measure and Lakshminarasu Chetty convened on the 9th April 1845 a meeting of the native inhabitants of Madras to draw up a memorial to the Supreme Government. The meeting was very largely attended and in pursuance of the unanimous resolution of the members a memorial was drawn up and sent to England complaining of the intended alteration in the law and protesting against the abrogation of the social and religious usages of the natives. The memorial reached the Supreme Government in due course and was accorded proper consideration. After some correspondence between the local and the Supreme Governments, the memorialists were informed that the obnoxious provisions of the enactment which had necessitated the memorial would be expunged from the Act.

The Missionaries next turned their attention to the Madras University. The Madras University which was started by Lord Elphinstone was giving Indian students a purely secular education. Missionaries and devoted friends of missionaries were engaged in testing year after year the progress that the students had made; they were often questioned on points connected with Christian theology and declared ineligible for appointments under the Government. When the natives murmured about such treatment they were quietly informed that the real panacea for these evils was the introduction of the Holy Bible as a text-book of studies.

Lakshminarasu Chetty convened again in

Pachaiyappa's institution a public meeting of Hindus on the 7th October 1846 over which he presided. It was resolved that a memorial be addressed to the Honorable the Court of Directors setting forth their grievances and praying for redress. A memorial was accordingly drawn up describing concisely the pledges which had been given ensuring the religious neutrality of Government, the unscrupulous violations of these sacred pledges during the regime of the Marquis of Tweeddale, the conversion policy of the missionaries, the active co-operation of Government officials with them, the apathy of the Governor in the matter of founding schools for the diffusion of European knowledge in the interior of the Presidency, the attempts of the missionaries to prevent the natives from passing competitive examinations, the disinclination of the local authorities to employ natives largely in offices under Government, the perversion of justice in courts owing to missionary influence and many other wrongs to which the natives were subjected. The deliberations of the meeting were thoroughly orderly and there was no trace of disloyalty or insubordination to the paramount power about them. Still it was alleged that the Chairman's address and the whole proceedings generally were calculated to foster a rebellious spirit in the audience and to wean the allegiance of the Hindus to their British Rulers. All that Lakshminarasu Chetty said was "we believe that by a mild and firm representation of our grievances to the superior authorities we shall obtain justice and redress." The Sheriff went out of his way to dissuade those assembled at the meeting from signing the memorial. But notwithstanding the intervention of the Sheriff more than twelve thousand peeple signed it. The memorial was forwarded through the local Government to the Honorable the Court of Directors and the local Government passed their own remarks upon the allegations contained in it, characterizing them as founded on utter ignorance of the doings of Government and on "partial extracts of official documents surreptitiously published." The memorial, we believe was shelved for the nonce in consideration of the observations of the Governor which accompanied it to the Honorable the Court of Directors. The attempt to introduce the Bible as a text book in Government schools was revived in 1853 but owing to the united efforts of George Norton, John Bruce Norton and Lakshminarasu Chetty, the scheme fell through.

In 1852 Mr. Danby Seymour, a member of the British Parliament, came out to India apparently for sight-seeing. At the time, the name of Lakshminarsu Chetty was well known to some Members of Parliament from the memorials now and then sent up under his guidance to England. On landing at Madras Mr. Seymour enquired of Lakshminarasu Chetty and from their very first acquaintance they became inspired with feelings of respect for each other. Mr. Seymour became Lakshminarasu Chetty's guest at Madras and the latter found very good opportuuities of conveying to Mr. Seymour information regarding the high-handed manner in which the local authorities curtailed the civil and religious rights of the Hindu community and regarding other serious defects in British Rule. Mr. Seymour accompanied by Lakshminarasu Chetty made a tour through Southern India visiting Cuddalore, Kumbakonam, Coimbatore and other places and learnt by personal observation how the landholder was assessed at prohibitive rates and how defaulters in the payment of Government revenue were subjected to excruciating torture and otherwise inhumanly treated. He saw unhappy men standing in the sun fully exposed to its scorching rays and with large stones resting on their backs performing under compulsion the penance and self-immolation which their forefathers voluntarily did in obedience to the regulations of the Sastras; some thumb-screwed and others tied down to adjacent trees and posts with their heads holding communion with their toes—and all this in front of the Taluq Cutcherry and within sight of the august Tahsildar and Magistrate who was holding his office and doing his work without wasting a thought on the unfortunate victims groaning inaudibly within a few yards of the Court house! Mr. Seymour took note of all that he had heard and seen about the malpractices of the officers and with a set of implements of torture neatly and safely bundled up left soon after for England.

In July 1854, on the occasion of a motion brought forward in the House of Commons, Mr. Seymour asserted that to his knowledge torture was inflicted on the natives of India not only in criminal cases under inquiry but also in the collection of revenue. This assertion was met by a distinct denial by several members in the House and conspicuous among them was Sir James Hogg who twitted Mr. Seymour with having gone into remote districts in the prosecution of vague and idle inquiries. Sir C. Wood who was President of the India Board at the time stated that he could not positively deny an accusation he had never heard before but he could cause a strict inquiry to be made. The report of the debate was sent out to India immediately and in September a Commission was appointed to inquire into the whole subject. In April following, the report was concluded and the whole mass of evidence was brought under the consideration of the Home Government. Meanwhile, Lakshminarasu Chetty caused a petition to be numerously signed and sent to Parliament and the Earl of Albemarle presented it to the House of Lords on the 14th April 1856. The House thereupon condemned the practice of torture in unmeasured terms.

In 1852, the Madras Native Association under the guidance of Lakshminarasu Chetty drafted a long and interesting petition detailing the grievances of the people of Southern India and presented it to Parliament. That petition premised by saying "that grievances of your petitioners arise principally from the excessive taxation and the vexations which accompany its collections, and the insufficiency, delays and expense of the Company's Courts of Law; that their chief wants are the construction of roads, bridges and works for the supply of irrigation and a better provision for the education of the people; they also desire a reduction of public expenditure and a form of local Government more generally conducive to the happiness of the subjects and the prosperity of the country." It concluded as follows:—"that in conclusion your petitioners would respectfully suggest that whether the Government of India be continued in the hands of the East India Company or otherwise provided for, the new system, whatever it may be, shall be open to alterations and improvements from time to time as the well-being of the country may require and that the working of its internal administration may undergo at stated interval, if practicable triennially but quinquennially at the latest, public enquiry and discussion in the Imperial Parliament in order that the people of this vast and distant empire may have more frequent opportunities of representing whatever grievances they seek to have redressed and that the local Governments may be stimulated to the diligent execution of their functions under the influence of a constant and efficient supervision of their conduct by the higher authorities at Home."

This petition was presented to the House of

Lords on the 25th February 1853 by the Earl of Ellenborough. The Earl of Albemarle in the course of a speech in the House of Lords in the same year on presenting a petition from the inhabitants of the city of Manchester praying that the future Government of India in England should consist of "a Minister and a Council appointed by the Crown and be directly responsible to the Imperial Parliament," said :—"He happened to have in his possession two letters confirmatory of the statements contained in the (Madras) petition from which he had just quoted. The letters were written by two thoroughly educated native gentlemen who were capable of giving expression to their ideas in as correct language as could be employed by any of their Lordships. The first of these gentlemen Lakshminarasu Chetty wrote as follows, uuder the date of Madras, January 24, 1853 :—'If a Commission could be obtained to take information in this country, all the more glaring complaints could be fully substantiated. We have tried to avoid exaggeration in our statements, but the evils alluded to are so great that nothing will convince people in Europe of their truth except the establishment of such Commission.'"

In the same year, John Bright made the following reference to the petition in the House of Commons :—"This petition is one of great length, is very ably drawn up and I may say I have seen several private letters from very influential persons in Madras, stating that if a Commission of Inquiry be sent out to the presidency they are prepared to establish every fact stated in the petition." The agitation was kept up in India by Lakshminarasu Chetty and in 1855, he sent another petition signed by 14,000 persons praying that the administration of the British Territories in India be transferred from the East India Company to the Crown. This petition was presented in the House of Lords by the Earl of Albemarle on the 16th July 1855. The agitation carried on by Lakshminarasu Chetty in Madras and others in Bombay and Bengal prior to 1853 had the effect of reducing the strength of the Court of Directors from thirty to eighteen of whom six were to be nominated by the Crown, of throwing the appointments in the Civil Service open to competition and of bringing about the amalgamation of the Company's Sadr Courts with the High Courts in the Presidency towns. The continuation of the agitation in subsequent years and the Mutiny in 1857 led to the extinction of the East India Company and the placing of India under the direct authority and control of Her Majesty the Queen in 1858.

So early as in 1854, Mr. J. B. Norton, in the course of his yearly address in Pachaiappa's Hall, expressed a hope that Lakshminarasu Chetty would soon become one of the Trustees of Pachaiappa's charities: "There is another gentleman also" he said, referring to Lakshminarasu Chetty "who will, I trust, ere long join you heartily in making common cause. He has been lately the subject of much animadversion and much misrepresentation; but both the sacrifices he has made in his purse and the labour and fatigue he has voluntarily undertaken in person testify forcibly to the practical interest which he takes in the welfare of his countrymen—I speak of Lakshminarasu Chetty." It is necessary to mention here that Lakshminarasu Chetty was about this period of his life regarded by the local authorities as a seditious person and a police watch was set over him. His speeches were closely scrutinised and his movements were watched by the police then as they do those of a known depredator now. Lakshminarasu Chetty was appointed a Trustee in 1854.

After the memorable Mutiny of 1857 Lakshminarasu Chetty as President of the Madras Native Association drew up a memorial to Government praying for the continuance of its policy of religious neutrality. The memorial was read with interest in England and fetched a satisfactory reply.

Meanwhile, the change in the executive officers of the Madras Government, the rising popularity of Lakshminarasu Chetty and the admiration of the European and Native communities for the self-sacrifices he had made on behalf of his country, made the Madras Government forget the odium in which he was once held. In recognition of the services he had rendered to his country, he was in 1861 made a C. S. I. and on the death of the Hon. V. Sadagopa Charlu in 1863 appointed a member of thc Madras Legislative Council. John Bruce

Norton alluding to this appointment in his address in Pachaiyappa's Hall in 1864 said that the Government had selected as Sadagopa Charlu's successor the man who would have been called to the post by the unanimous suffrage of his fellow-countrymen.

Lakshminarasu Chetty had, in the meanwhile, directed his attention to the state of affairs in Mysore. In the war with Tippu, the English had received considerable aid from the Nizam and there was a sort of compact between the English and their ally that in the event of the English not restoring the province of Mysore to the Native Raja, it should be parcelled out fairly between the English and the Nizam. Lakshminarasu Chetty who had marked the reluctance of Englishmen in India to restore Mysore to Krishna Raj Udayar went to Mysore and advised the old Rajah to adopt a son for the perpetuation of his family and press for the recognition of the rights of the adopted son by the Home Government. At the same time, he prevailed upon Sir Salar Jung, the famous Minister of Hyderabad, to assert the claims of the Nizam to a fair moiety of Mysore if the British Government were not willing to restore Mysore to the Native Raja. We need hardly add that English statesmen who saw that in conformity to their pledge they should either restore Mysore to the Native Raj, or failing that, parcel it out and give a moiety to the Nizam under the compact, resolved upon the more honorable expedient of recognizing the rights of the adopted son of Krishna Raj Udayar to succeed to the throne on attaining his majority. With the aid of John Bruce Norton, Lakshminarasu Chetty also made strong efforts to place the widows of the late Raja of Tanjore in a prosperous condition and to relieve the sufferings of the family of the last Nabob of the Carnatic after his death.

By this time, *i.e.*, 1864, Lakshminarasu Chetty had ceased to be wealthy. The *Crescent* with its highly paid establishment had considerably drained his resources; the family trade was almost a losing concern and his son, to whom Lakshminarasu Chetty had for some years entrusted the management of his firm had brought it to ruin. The *Crescent* was given up for want of funds; and Lakshminarasu Chetty continued poor for the rest of his life. He died in 1868 leaving a name for genuine patriotism and self-sacrifice rare in the annals of India.

Referring to his death, John Bruce Norton said in the course of his address at Pachaiyappa's Hall in 1869. "He was for many years one of my closest personal friends; I know of none whose memory I more esteem. It is not of my own personal loss that I have now to speak; it is of the general loss which the community has sustained by the death of this great and good man. Possessed of excellent abilities, highly educated, with refined taste, and a most powerful judgment, he was the best type of a true patriot, not a noisy demagogue but one who appealed only to the legal, peaceable weapons of reason; he, years ago dedicated his talents and his fortune to the service of his countrymen at a time when the task was more difficult, if not dangerous, than what it is to-day. It requires no small courage for a native to start and sustain a journal devoted to the interests of native society. It caused him far more evil than good report. He sacrificed a large portion of his patrimony in the patriotic object he had in view. No one who remembers the *Crescent* will deny that it was written with much force of argument and close logical reasoning and that its temper was generally calm and dignified. That it did much towards bringing about the recognition of the social and political rights of the natives, I cannot doubt. When he was nominated to the honorable post of a member of the Legislative Council, every one felt, whatever might be the divisions between this and that section of Native Society, that he was the best representative man who could have been selected. A retiring disposition, perhaps, somewhat impeded his nsefulness, but when he died, all felt that he had left a void that cannot be supplied. A meeting was at once held to consider how honor could best be shown to his memory: and it was determined that a public subscription should be raised for the purpose of placing his picture in this Hall, and founding a Sanscrit Scholarship in his name in the Presidency College. Believe me, in honoring such a man's memory you honor yourselves. I do not doubt that a large subscription will be forthcoming for carrying out these objects. The Maharajah of Travancore, the First Prince, and the Dewan Sir Madava Row, whose names are ever coupled with all that is enlightened and generous, I hear, have sent in their subscriptions and condolences. Many native gentlemen have subscribed, and though we are not so wealthy as the munificent Native merchants of Bombay before ruin overtook their city, I cannot doubt as to the success of this proposition to honour so great and good a man."

Mr. Norton again paid a handsome compliment to Lakshminarasu Chetty in 1870 in the following words :—"With respect to that (the portrait) of the Honorable Lakshminarasu Chetty, in the words of the report, I feel that it is superfluous to speak. At the same time, I cannot help stating that I hold in my hand a copy of a letter from one native to another, speaking of him in the very highest terms, as the originator of enquiry into almost every abuse and defects which formerly marked the administration of this country; a letter which is above all suspicion, as it shows in what estimation the natives themselves hold his memory. I have no time to read it to you; I must content myself with observing that he was a zealous and honest reformer and that he backed his convictions by putting his hand into his pocket in their support. He founded the *Crescent*, a journal which, under the able Mr. Harley, for years advocated the Native cause. In this undertaking, Lakshminarasu Chetty sunk a very considerable portion of his fortunes; in 1852, at the renewal of the Charter, he drew up the Native petition, which was assailed at the time as a tissue of mis-statements, but which certainly contributed very largely to those numerous enquiries into the practice of torture, over-assessment, and the like, which shortly followed; while the general respect in which he was held by the Government during the latter portion of his life, proves that the part he played in his earlier political career was so truthful and sincere. He received at the hands of the Queen the honour of a Companionship of the Star of India, and when he was selected by the Government as a member of the Legislative Council, all sections of Native Society unanimously felt that he was the best representative of Native opinion. He was snatched away just when he was likely to have become most useful. He was so singularly modest and retiring that these qualities somewhat perhaps even impaired his utility to the public. He was a man of the keenest intellect and of the most kindly disposition. He was a staunch supporter of the cause of education. All admit that the void his loss has caused cannot be supplied."

Lakshminarasu Chetty, though he belonged more to the first half of this century was by no means a Conservative in social matters. He had great faith in the education of women. He started and provided several Girls' schools at his own expense and advocated and even encouraged the marriage of widows. His sympathies were always with the agricultural classes. He loved and cultivated the society of educated men whether Tamil and Telugu Pundits or English Scholars and privately helped many a young man in prosecuting his studies. In fact, he staked the whole of his fortune in his noble and patriotic attempt to ameliorate the political and social condition of his countrymen.

RAI BAHADUR S. RAMASAWMY MUDALIAR, M.A., B.L.

Rai Bahadur Salem Ramasawmi Mudaliar was born in Salem on the 6th September 1852. He belonged to a highly respected family in Salem. Venkatachala Mudaliar, the great-grandfather of Ramasawmi Mudaliar was an Agent or Dubash of the East India Company and Ramasawmi Mudaliar's father, Salem Gopalasawmi Mudaliar, is an influential Mittadar or extensive landowner, in Salem. He was Tahsildar of Namkal and retired on pension in 1867.

At the early age of six, Ramasawmi was sent to Madras for education. His guardian in Madras was one Nagalinga Mudaliar, son of a well-known Tamil scholar, Conjeveram Sabapathy Mudaliar. The man who had charge of his vernacular education was one Kathirvelu Vadyar, a wit and a pandit. Ramasawmi in course of time joined the Madras High School, now the Presidency College, from which he was sent to Pachaiappa's School on the abolition of the primary classes in the former institution. After reaching the required standard he was sent back to the Presidency College, where he completed his educational course.

In the Presidency Collge, Ramasawmi studied diligently, winning the esteem of his Professors and carrying off several prizes. At the Matriculation examination, he obtained one of the Government scholarships awarded to the first fifteen successful candidates. He was also the first of his year at the First in Arts Examination. The subjects in which he distinguished himself were Tamil, English Composition and History. He passed the B.A. Examination in 1871 as first in the Presidency. Mr. Thompson, the then Principal of the Presidency College had such a high opinion of the ability, industry and good conduct of Ramasawmy that on his graduation he offered him an Assistant Professorship of English at the College—a place which he declined with the object of allowing the offer to be made to the next man who, he knew, was in sore need of help. He then followed up his studies at the College by preparing in private for the Degree of Master of Arts in History and Moral Science, which he obtained in 1873. In 1875, he qualified himself for the legal profession. At the B. L., Examination too he stood first in the list of passed candidates. At the recommendation of Mr. Justice Holloway, Ramsawmy Mudaliar was trained as an Apprentice-at-Law by the Hon. Mr. P. O'Sullivan. In 1876 he was enrolled as a High Court Vakil and established himself at Salem for practising there.

By his unassuming manners and the sensible way in which he conducted his cases, he won the respect and good will of the native community and the esteem of the District Judge at Salem. At the same time, the general turn of his mind rendered him fitter for the bench than for the bar. With a view to use his talents in the service of Government, he sought a place in the Judicial Department. The application was endorsed by the District Judge who was "happy to be able to express an opinion that he is well qualified both as to legal attainments, and, what in my opinion is still more important, as to character." He was appointed a District Munsiff in the Trichinopoly District in 1876. His judicial administration was marked by the most thorough-going honesty and the strictest impartiality. He regarded it as a sacred duty always to maintain an independent judgment in the discharge of his official functions. If anybody attempted to bring outside influence to bear upon him he resented it as an insult. A story is told of how one of the parties in a case which he was to decide in his court brought "a letter of recommendation" or introduction, to the Munsiff from a person for whom he had great regard. The party thus introduced was received politely and all due kindness shown to him. The Munsiff even drove him to the court with him. But vain and mistaken were the party's hopes if he thought on these grounds, as indeed he did think, that the case would be decided in his favour. On taking his seat, the Munsiff delivered judgment; and the party did not wait to be taken home by the Munsiff. More than once he spoke from the bench against these letters of introduction, pointing out the futility as well as the wickedness of such tamperings with the course of justice. Thus he held on to the path of rectitude he had chosen without swerving either to the right or to the left. The work was as hard as he was conscientious; and the responsibility was great. He had once to recoup to Government a portion of the money lost through defalcation in his office.

He, however, did not continue long on the bench. He felt that the public service did not afford a free field for distinction. Though disappointed in his hopes, his service as Munsiff gave him a high place in the esteem of the native community as is evidenced by the following testimony of Mr. A. Seshiah Sastri, the late Dewan of Pudukotta: "Though I have not the pleasure of a personal acquaintanee with Salem Ramasawmy Mudaliar, M. A., B. L., of the Madras University, I have always heard the very best accounts of him as District Munsiff of Udiarpallium. His unassuming manners, his strict impartiality, and his integrity, have won for him the confidence of the people nnder his jurisdiction. I have always considered him one of the best young men of whom the University may be proud, and who is destined to rise high in the service which he has entered." Destined! He was not so destined. After having offered to resign twice before, he finally gave up service under Government in 1882. He resolved to practise at Madras.

In the High Court, he generally appeared on the Appellate Side and when he took up original cases, he was supported by a junior. His knowledge of law was soon recognized as sound. Though others might excel him in the subtlety with which they could draw legal distinctions, none had a firmer or truer grasp of the principles of law. He was endowed, as it were, with an instinct which rendered him sensitive to every discord in the internal harmony of the judicial science. With him Law was not a mere means of livelihood; his enthusiasm for its study led him to start the *Law Journal* of which he was Chief Editor till 1891. His legal attainments were recognised by the University who appointed him Examiner for the B.L. and the M.L. Examinations. His scholarship in Tamil Literature was utilized for the Examinations for the B. A. Degree. In 1887, he was appointed a Fellow of the Madras University. His services were highly valued by the Faculties of Law and of Arts; of both of which faculties he was a member.

In the events which have made the India of the present politically different from the India of 1880, Ramasawmy Mudaliar played an effective part. In South India, at all events, none had such a single eye for the general good as he. As during his official days he resisted private influences in the discharge of his judicial functions, so in his later days when he was answerable to none but himself, he preserved his judgment untainted by party prejudice or class interest. At the same time, his zeal for the public cause was none the less warm nor his position any the less pronounced. The first time he took a prominent part in a public movement was in 1882 for protesting against any public character being accorded to a memorial meeting in honor of a retiring Councillor, Mr. D. F. Carmichael.

During the first years of the last decade, India passed through a political ferment under the regime of a Viceroy whose well-known popular sympathies were resisted by the fury of a powerful community which felt itself outraged thereby. The Ilbert Bill agitation stirred the smooth waters of Indian politics to the very depths. In Madras, the people were ruled by a Governor who boasted of his ignorance of public opinion and who lavished public money on extravagant adornments of his own residence on the hills. Sensible of the feeble hand that held the reins, officials throughout the Presidency had their own sweet way; and one scandal after another broke out in different parts. During all this time much had to be done by way of vigilantly guarding the interests and persistently urging the claims of the people. The greater security there now is against official vagaries, and the greater willingness with which Anglo-Indians admit the claims of natives to an increasing share in the Government of the country, have been brought about in Madras, at least partially, by the agitation carried on by the Mahajana Sabha; and among its members, it is an open secret that Salem Ramasawmy Mudaliar exercised considerable influence. When the history of that agitation in South India comes to be written as it deserves to be, it will be seen how much the loyalty, the moderation, the practical as opposed to the merely sentimental, the generous as opposed to the merely narrow and selfish, character of the movement was due to the wise part which Salem Ramasawmy Mudaliar took in its counsels. In the Salem Riots case,—when an attempt was made to include his father, as an influential Mittadar, among those implicated in the trouble, although his father, was at the time of the riots in Madras,—he declined a brief to defend the prisoners that he might more effectively work in extra-professional ways for procuring their freedom.

One happy and effective way that suggested itself to the political leaders in India for the redress of the people's grievances soon after Lord Ripon's departure, was that some of India's own sons should go to England and plead her cause before the English voters at the General Election of 1885. For this responsible and novel task, Salem Ramasawmy Mudaliar was deputed to England from Madras with two other delegates from Bombay and Bengal. Ramasawmy Mudelliar and his brother delegates addressed several meetings in England. They visited London first and then they sallied forth to Swansea in Wales, to Newcastle-on-Tyne, to Birmingham and to Aberdeen in the north of Scotland. At their first appearance in London at the Westbourne chapel, we are told of "an earnest politician, a girl of nineteen evidently a working girl whose umbrella, none too strong at the begining of the meeting, seemed likely to be shaken to pieces by the hard concussions with which she sought to indicate her enthusiasm."

At Birmingham, the delegates spoke at a liberal gathering held in support of the candidature of John Bright. Ramasawmy Mudaliar considered the meeting at which Mr. Bright spoke on India, the greatest he had ever attended. Mr. Chamberlain also took part in this demonstration. On his way to Aberdeen, Ramasawmy Mudaliar halted at Edinburgh where he fulfilled his object of hearing Mr. Gladstone who spoke at the great Music Hall. The meetings in Aberdeen formed a fitting climax to the political mission of Ramasawmy Mudaliar in Great Britain. Dr. W. A. Hunter and Professor Bryce availed themselves of the presence of Ramasawmy Mudaliar to form in the "Granite City," an association for the diffusion of knowledge about India.

Thus was brought to a close the "campaign" of the Indian delegates. The effect of these meetings on the English mind generally was a profound impression of the overwhelming responsibility borne by England towards this country. Ramasawmy Mudaliar individually made on English audiences an impression which was quite unique. His personal appearance was to them somewhat romantic. "A fine handsome face, with large black eyes, such as Moore has painted in

Lallah Rookh, with as finely chiselled a face as you could find in the lobbies of the law-Courts"—such was the picture of the man as it fell on the English retina. His mode of speaking was as strongly marked as his personal appearance. There was in his words a quiet dignity and force peculiar to the man himself. The simple earnestness of his voice carried conviction with it; and the foreign accent which was detectable in his delivery heightened the impression it made. His English tour effected a great improvement in Ramasawmi Mudaliar's style of public speaking. Between his first speech at Westbourne and his last one at Aberdeen, there was all the difference there is between the tracing on set forms in a copy book and a free hand. But what carried his words straight to the heart of his English hearers was the pathetic appeal for confidence and sympathy which underlay all his remarks. He spoke about financial retrenchment by reducing the army and enlisting native volunteers, about giving the sons of the soil a larger share in the administration of the country and about reducing taxation and thus relieving the poverty of the ryots. These were grievances to be redressed; but in communicating them there was not the slightest suggestion of discontent. On the other hand, Ramasawmy Mudaliar felt and expressed his conviction, that while England could do without India, India could not do without England.

It may not be generally known that Ramasawmy Mudaliar in his trip to England tried to avoid doing anything by which his place amongst his caste men might be forfeited. He went a Hindu and came back a Hindu, taking a Hindu servant with him who cooked his food. He declined invitations to meat dinners while he participated in vegetable food with English friends. Thus he did nothing in England which he dared not avow among the men of his community by whom he was taken back without a murmur,—and without the humiliating rite of *prayischittam*. On his return, he met with an enthusiastic reception from the native public of Madras. His self-effacing humility on that occasion only served to show the true magnitude and value of the services rendered by him to the country at large. His reception at Salem was if possible even more enthusiastic, though it could not have been more appreciative.

Yet another task awaited the England-returned delegate of the Madras Presidency. The persistent demand of educated natives for a larger share in the work of governing the country, led to the appointment in 1886 of the Public Service Commission to which he was appointed as the representative of the non-official community of Madras. Other Hindu members of the Commission were Sir Romesh Chunder Mitter of Bengal, the Hon. K. L. Nulkar of Bombay and the Rajah of Bhinga. Sir Charles Aitchison was the President. It was urged from the beginning by the official members that the adoption of the Commission's recommendations by Government and the Secretary of State would depend upon those recommendations being made unanimously. But the interests represented on the Commission were mutually irreconcilable; and compromise was but partial surrender. The action of the native members in not having stood up for the Civil Service Examinations being held simultaneously in England and India by writing a dissenting minute in favour of them, has been adversedly criticised by leaders of native opinion, but with the disagreement that existed among the native members, it was thought best not to press the point on Government, even by means of a dissenting minute. This was the explanation which Ramasawmy Mudaliar himself submitted to the National Congress at Allahabad in 1888.

Though Ramasawmy Mudaliar attended but two Congresses, the one at Madras in 1887 when he hurried down from his labours on the Public Service Commission at Calcutta just in time to take part in the debate on the Arms Act and the other at Allahabad, his services to the Congress cause were felt to be so valuable that its Presidentship was once offered to him—an honour which he declined because he thought he had not sufficiently established a claim thereto. With him it was not a shrinking from responsibility but an inherent bashfulness towards outward honour.

As a Trustee of Pachaiappa's Charities, he did effectual work. On the Madras Municipal Board his counsel was valued both by the President and the Commissioners; and if it had been given to him to witness the fruition of his political labours connected with the Indian Councils Act of 1893, he would have been returned by that body to the Legislative Council. In the meantime, Death by whom so many of the promising men of this country are carried away before they attain the meridian of their power claimed him and he passed away on the 2nd March 1892.

By his death, Hindu Society lost the silent charm of his character. It was often remarked that there were two men—Professor Runganadam and Salem Ramasawmy—who by their inspiring presence, dignified manners and edifying conversation, made the Cosmopolitan Club genial and attractive. If one was like the flower which by unfolding its petals sheds light and fragrance around, the other was like the bud whose very form is a picture of modesty concealing beauty and sweetness within. But Ramasawmy Mudelliar's claim to be remembered by posterity rests not on his social influence, or his legal erudition, or even on the unassuming sincerity of his character amid a generation that is fast losing its ancestral Hindu virtues and adopting the artificial insincerities of Western civilization but on the fact that he was a model of a Hindu public man.

Ramasawmy Mudaliar had hidden beneath his meekness, a certain dogged assertiveness. This is a quality which when unsupported by sound judgment degenerates into obstinacy, but which when based on keen insight constitutes the stuff of which heroes are made. In his case, it was the secret of the steady unostentatious perseverence which characterised his life. It saved his mildness from any appearance of a desire to please. He was plain, straightforward and sincere. His language was never in advance of his purpose nor his purpose too much in advance of his ability. He was humble but he could rebuke. He was charitable in his judgment of others: but he would not condone their faults. He was independent, though not forward; and when he submitted to the will of others, he did so deliberately. The sweet reasonableness that marked his intercourse was as much a matter of will as of temperament.

C. V. RUNGA CHARLU, C.I.E.

Cettipaniam Veeravalli Runga Charlu was born in 1831 in a village in the Chingleput District. He was the son of C. Ragava Chariar, a clerk in the Chingleput Collectorate. While he was yet a child he narrowly escaped an accident. The cart in which his mother travelled capsized and he escaped from serious peril to his life and limbs only by his removal from the lap of his mother by her brother, just a moment before the collapse of the cart. Runga Charlu's father, besides his small pay, had no property of any kind. He was anxious to give his son a good English education, but his very slender resources had almost compelled him to give up the idea, when happily for Runga Charlu one of his paternal uncles died at the time, bequeathing a small sum of Rs. 800 to be laid out upon his education. This was no doubt a material addition to the resources of his father, but was hardly large enough to ensure his being sent to Madras for education. His father was still undecided, but the timely offer of patronage and help by V. Raghava Chariar, the first native Magistrate in Madras removed all his father's apprehensions, and Runga Charlu was sent to Madras for education.

As a school-boy, Runga Charlu had the reputation of being precocious. He would often sit near his grown up kinsmen silently watching them play at chess, and he became such an adept in this royal game that when any of the players got puzzled by some difficult move, they would consult their boy companion for a solution, which they readily obtained. Runga Charlu when a school boy paid more attention to play than to his books; but he was so remarkably intelligent that with far less devotion to study he was able to distance most of his classmates. He was at first educated in Pachaiappa's School and his first teacher happened to be one Priya-gnana Mudaliar. He always loved and reverenced his old tutor and through all the latter years of his life he set him up as a model to those who undertook the teaching of infant classes in the Madras and Mysore Schools. During the last years of his life when age incapacitated the teacher for school work his loyal pupil periodically rendered him pecuniary help.

Runga Charlu was next sent to the Madras High School and Mr. Powell who found in him a bright and promising student gave him a scholarship of fourteen Rupees a month which he accepted. Under Mr. Powell's teaching his intellect expanded and he so thoroughly distanced his fellow-students, that their highest ambition was to be but second to him. He continued his course in the Madras High School till the beginning of 1849, when he passed the Proficient's test with great credit, obtaining a first class certificate. Mr. Powell had such a high opinion of Runga Charlu that subsquently when he declared his intention of competing for a Public Examination, Mr. Powell wrote to him, "I feel personally obliged to you for having made up your mind to enter the lists and throw down your glove on behalf of this institution . . . . you have ability, added to it energy and judgment and you are sure to succeed."

His brilliant career at school and the reputation which his high intelligence had already earned for him so favorably impressed Mr. Ellis of the Madras Civil Service that he appointed him almost immediately after he left school, as a clerk in the Madras Collectorate; and ere the term of acting appointment had expired he was confirmed as a clerk in the Chingleput Collectorate. From Chingleput, be was transferred on promotion to Salem where he became Head Writer. About this time he published two pamphlets, one on "Bribery and Corruption in the Revenue Department" and the other on the then burning question of "Mirasi Rights in the Chingleput and Tanjore Districts." Runga Charlu's next promotion was as Tahsildar of Saidapet, which office he held for two years. From Saidapet he was transferred to Nellore as next in rank to the Sheristadar in that Collectorate and was soon made Head Sheristadar. In 1859, he was appointed Special Assistant to Mr. G. N. Taylor, the President of the newly organised Inam Commission for the Madras Presidency. Runga Charlu distinguished himself by his ability and integrity and won the confidence of Mr. Taylor. His service in this department extended over a period of about seven years.

When Mr. Taylor's work on the Inam Commission was brought to a termination, the Madras Government appointed him to the special duty of enquiring into and reporting on the working of the Indian Railways. And he chose Runga Charlu as his coadjutor in his new sphere of work which required an intimate knowledge of accounts. Runga Charlu accepted the offer without consulting even his best friends and dearest relatives, but on going home an attempt was made to dissuade him from keeping his word with Mr. Taylor. The engagement involved a voyage to Calcutta. It was urged that a high class Brahmin like Runga Charlu would be setting a most objectionable precedent by sailing in a ship to Calcutta. But Runga Charlu was far in advance of the times and cared not a jot for the terrors of ex-communication. He followed Mr. Taylor to Calcutta and other places where their business called them, giving fresh proofs of his honesty and high intellect and strengthening the very favourable impression which he had produced on the mind of his superior. His duties having been faithfully and satisfactorily discharged, he returned to Madras. Mr. Taylor's appreciation of Runga Charlu is best expressed in the following extract from a letter of Mr. Taylor :—

"We were on terms of the closest intercourse from the period of his leaving College and entering public service in 1849 and our mutual regard never faltered to the last. Whatever he may have owed to me for a helping hand at first starting or for subsequent advancement in the public service was amply repaid by steady and untiring devotion. Throughout the whole of our official intercourse, his intimate knowledge of native character, his excellent judgment, his wonderful capacity for affairs and his able and ungrudging assistance were always at my disposal. I attribute, in short, to his constant and ready help, whatever of success I may have accomplished in the several measures with which we were associated." Mr. Taylor who afterwards became the Madras member of the Viceroy's Council, consulted Runga Charlu and quoted in the Council his opinions with reference to the various legislative measures introduced into the Council. After his return to Madras, Runga Charlu was appointed Commissioner in the Madras Railway Company. On the organization of the Currency Department in 1864 he was appointed Treasury Deputy Collector at Calicut, where he won the esteem of Mr. G. Ballard, the Collector, who afterwards became British Resident of Travancore and Cochin.

Meanwhile, affairs in Mysore were undergoing a complete revolution. The adopted son of the dethroned Kristna Raj Woodyar was recognised as heir to the throne and it was resolved that the kingdom should be handed over to him on his attaining the age of eighteen. It was further resolved that, to prevent the recurrence of any catastrophe such as had necessitated the interference of even Lord William Bentinck, the well-known advocate of peace and the non-interference policy in India, the young Maharajah should be given an education and a training which would fit him for undertaking the onerous responsibilities of a king with five millions of subjects and for administering the kingdom in a manner conducive to the material prosperity and well-being of his subjects. This order of the Secretary of State for India necessitated an immediate revolution in the administration of the province. Mr. L. Bowring, who was then in charge of Mysore on behalf of the British Government, wrote to Mr. Ellis for a trustworthy Madrasi to hold the appointment of Comptroller of the Mysore palace. Runga Charlu was recommended for the place. He accepted the offer and joined the Mysore service in 1868. Soon after taking up his appointment, he was deputed, without prejudice to his duties as Comptroller, to assist Major Elliot in preparing an account of the moveable property of the palace, giving the estimated value of every item of property and to arrange for the safe custody of the more valuable portion of them, consisting chiefly of costly ornaments belonging to the Raja.

Runga Charlu next directed his attention to

the confused state of affairs within the palace. With the small executive powers which his position gave him, he checked the growing malpractices within the palace walls. He rid the palace of a large number of useless sycophants who were fattening upon the palace resources. Col. Malleson was at this time the Tutor and Guardian of the Mysore Prince and the able and affective way in which Runga Charlu cleansed the palace of all wicked underlings enlisted the sympathy of Malleson. The following letter addressed to Runga Charlu by the Colonel shows how highly he esteemed Runga Charlu: "I have been struck with the noble tone of your letter. It went quite to my heart. I am very glad of your determination to come to Ooty with the Maharajah. I can easily conceive that you must be tired. You are the brain and life of our concern and I cannot say how much I am indebted to you."

In 1874, Runga Charlu published in London a remarkable pamphlet entitled 'The British Administration of Mysore.' The author promised the public another pamphlet which was to contain suggestions for the future. But this was never given to the world and the only probable reason of this breach of promise is that Runga Charlu was soon raised to a position where he had free scope and sufficient authority to put into immediate practice the suggestions he had intended to make. This pamphlet was no sooner published in Mysore than its author ceased to be regarded as a mere Comptroller of the palace. He was universally recognised as a man of consummate ability. Mr. Gordon, Chief Commissioner of Mysore, chose Runga Charlu as his Revenue Secretary. They jointly introduced several reforms and changes which considerably reduced the expenditure previously incurred. A Native Secretary and Revenue Commissioner was substituted for three Commissioners, who were previously discharging the same functions. The salary of Deputy Commissioners, which originally ranged from Rs. 1,000 to1,666 was reduced to the grade of Rs.700 to 1,000. The offices of eight of the twenty-seven Assistant Commissioners were abolished. All European Assistant Commissioners drawing large salaries were replaced by nineteen natives on moderate pay. All except four of the Deputy Commissioners receiving the old scale of salary were removed and efficient natives appointed instead. Similar reforms upon the principle of substituting cheap but efficient natives for highly paid Europeans were inaugurated in every branch of the administration, *viz.*, the Educational, the Forest and the Public Works Departments. Owing to these reductions and other numerous items of retrenchment in other directions, the expenditure for the year 1879-80, the first year of Runga Charlu's Secretaryship, was two lakhs and a half short of the actual receipts for the year. It will thus be seen that in the course of one short year of his being raised to the Revenue Secretaryship, Runga Charlu was able, under the superintendence and co-operation of Mr. Gordon, to institute reforms and to reduce expenditure.

In appreciation of these services the Government of India honored him with the title of C.I.E. in 1880. But some of the natives of Mysore were resolved to decry his intellectual accomplishments and even to traduce his unimpeachable moral character. In 1880 it was alleged for the first time in public prints that some jewels were clandestinely removed from the palace by somebody in 1872 or 1873 and it was suggested that the then Comptroller of the Palace had certainly much to answer for in that connection. False as this and kindred allegations apparently were, they created quite a sensation at the time in Mysore. Mr. Bowring, at whose instance, Runga Charlu was taken to Mysore and who reported in terms of unqualified praise of Runga Charlu's work as Assistant to Major Elliot, thought that an explanation was then due from him to the Mysore public and hastened to write to one of the Mysore officials letters exculpating himself. "When I nominated him (Runga Charlu) on the recommendation of the Madras Government to assist Major Elliot," wrote Mr. Bowring on the 25th August 1880, to a Mysore official, "it was not my intention that he should assume a high administrative position, for I regarded his appointment as of a temporary character, while recent events would have disinclined me still more from selecting him as Dewan." In another letter dated 30th December 1880, to the same Mysore correspondent he said: "As regards the introduction into Mysore of Mr. Runga Charlu, I am responsible for it as you remark; but you know that

I nominated him for a special purpose and that it never entered into my head that he would assume the prominent position he now holds. Perhaps you will say that I ought to have foreseen this, but in reply I may urge that, had I remained Chief Commissioner, I would not have allowed him to exercise any undue sway in the country. I cannot regret having obtained his services to assist Major Elliot, for his work in this capacity was very well done; but I do not hold myself responsible for his subsequent self-aggrandisement. Supposing an engineer constructed an irrigation channel, and that owing to want of attention on the part of his successor the channel ate into its banks and flooded the country, would you hold the first man responsible? I think not; so I cannot take blame to myself for any unchecked action on Mr. Runga Charlu's part. If he be nominated Dewan, it will not be in accordance with my suggestion."

In justice to Mr. Bowring, it is necessary to add here what he thought of Runga Charlu at the time of his death. "I hasten to convey my sincere sympathy on an event which besides the great sorrow which it must naturally cause to the members of his family is to be deplored as a national misfortune by the people of Mysore. I am well aware of the efforts made by him to restore the financial position of the provinces and of the laudable steps taken by him to promote the welfare of its inhabitants who, by his untimely death, have lost a sincere benefactor and a wise administrator. I feel very anxious for the future of the country, as although there are doubtless many able officials from among whom the selection of a successor might be made, I fear there is no one in the Province who is likely to command the support both of the Resident and the Maharajah. Administrative talent combined with integrity and a knowledge of character is a rare accomplishment. Rare, indeed, are integrity and patriotism."

The supposed disappearance of the palace jewels was thoroughly and satisfactorily explained by Mr. Wilson and other respectable officials. The whole affair was traced to a mere clerical error for which Runga Charlu was certainly not responsible, and the other allegations against the character and intellectual qualifications of Runga Charlu were proved to be altogether baseless and malicious. On the 25th March 1881 he was appointed Dewan of Mysore.

To form a reasonable estimate of the success of Runga Charlu's administration as Dewan of the province of Mysore it is necessary to take into consideration its financial, agricultural and industrial condition at the time of the rendition. Expensive establishments in every branch of the administration after the model of the adjacent British dominions had well-nigh drained the resources of the country and the terrible famine of 1877 almost unprecedented in the annals of any province in India for its severity impoverished the exchequer. A million of the people whom it affected had succumbed to its effects and as the major portion of these unfortunate victims were sturdy men who earned by handicraft more than they consumed, their deaths produced a retarding influence on the extent and success of handicraft for some years to come. The amount of immediate damage caused by the terrible famine to produce, live stock and other property was estimated at ten millions sterling. The comparatively small saving effected by judicious reforms and the inauguration of a policy of retrenchment during the official years 1878, 1879, and 1880 was more than swallowed up by the special and additional expenditure incurred during the close of the official year 1880 under the heads of installation and palace charges and a few expensive reforms that had necessarily to be instituted despite the poverty of the State. The revenue which before the famine was nearly a hundred and ten lakhs a year, was just recovering itself and there was not the slightest possibility of any addition to it by increased taxation. The industrial activity of Mysore had considerably abated after the famine. The standing debt of eighty lakhs due by the State to the Imperial Government drained the country of 4 lakhs of rupees annually by way of interest. It was under such circumstances which would have daunted the sanguine spirit of the best of statesmen that Runga Charlu began his career as Dewan of Mysore. The only advantage which Runga Charlu possessed was the intelligent appreciation and co-operation of the young Maharaja who, though too young to lead had grown old enough to be worthily led.

The first task that engaged his attention was the completion of the reforms which had been inaugurated by the Mysore Commission and partially achieved during the two preceding years. Hassan and Chittaldroog ceased to be separate districts for the purpose of civil and criminal administration. Nine taluks were converted into Deputy Amildars' stations: four Munsiffs' Courts and three Sub-Courts were abolished: five out of eight District Jails were also abolished, as also the establishments attached to a number of travellers' bungalows. All these reductions resulted in considerable savings to the extent of nearly 2 lakhs of rupees annually. Runga Charlu next directed his attention chiefly to the Forest Department which, owing to maladministration and to some extent the nature of the country and the difficulties of traffic, had not been yielding a revenue commensurate with the area covered by the forests and the demand for timber. The long-established custom of disallowing the sale of sandal and the wasting of all available quantity of it within the four walls of the palace was discontinued and the revenue from the Forest Department showed a considerable increase.

With the help of savings thus effected, Runga Charlu made the long talked of Mysore Railway, an accomplished fact with an outlay of eleven lakhs of Rupees. There was no reform so highly appreciated by Runga Charlu as the introduction of a network of railways within the Mysore territory affording considerable facilities for communication and for the development of local industries by connecting Mysore with the outlying districts of the British dominions. Mysore possessed all facilities for purposes of irrigation, but still a large area of land remained uncultivated and a larger area ill-cultivated. This defect in the agricultural industry of Mysore, Runga Charlu discovered was attributable not to want of conveniences of irrigation but to want of enterprise in the agricultural portion of the population. And this defect could only be cured by the introduction of railways. Notwithstanding the crippled resources of the country, Runga Charlu met the expenditure required for the construction of the railway without making it felt as a grievance. He more than once assured the Representative Assembly that year after year a sum of five lakhs would be allotted to meet the expenditure incurred by the construction of railways until the proposed line of communication should have been accomplished.

The next important subject that attracted his attention was the heavy debt of eighty lakhs which the State owed to the Imperial Government. The state of finances negatived all hopes of the debt being paid off in a lump for ages following. The interest on the amount of the debt was in itself a startling figure and for a nnmber of years it would be as much as the State could do to be punctually paying up the interest. As matters stood, the payment of the debt could be demanded at any moment by the Imperial Government and the State would, in that contingency, be driven at the best to adopt measures altogether ruinous to its prosperity. With the object, therefore, of providing against such a contingency and of securing such other concessions as the Imperial Government might in their generous wisdom be induced to grant, he opened correspondence with the British Government, laying stress not merely on the impoverished condition of Mysore, but on the confessed mismanagement of the famine-relief works while the country was under British administration —a fact admitted by Lord Lytton, the then Viceroy of India. The result of the correspondence was that very favorable terms were granted to the State. The interest was reduced from five to four per cent. (no small concession where the capital was eighty lakhs) and the loan itself was made payable in forty-one annual instalments of four lakhs. This arrangement reduced the enormous debt to an increased expenditure of four lakhs a year for forty-one years.

All apprehensions on the subject of this enormous debt having been set at rest by this arrangement, Runga Charlu directed his attention to the funds required for the construction of the line from Bangalore to Tiptur. Encumbered as the State was he would not abandon this project or even postpone it; but with commendable boldness that rested on calculations of profit which the line was expected to bring in, he applied for and obtained the permission of the British Government to raise a loan of the sum necessary to be laid out on the line. A loan of 20 lakhs was raised and the construction of the line was begun and pushed on energetically.

But we have yet to speak of the most glorious feature of Runga Charlu's administration of Mysore. It was the organization of the Representative Assembly. The statesmanlike caution with which Runga Charlu approached this experiment as it must then have appeared to every body cannot but raise our estimate of his intellectual powers and foresight. The Representative Assembly was not to be given any active share in the administration of the province. The members were to be mere recipients of information about the doings of Government and of its intentions with regard to the future. They were assured that the Government had the best interests of its subjects at heart and that it would try to promote their prosperity. The provisions of new laws intended to be introduced would be explained to them that they might see their utility. It was necessary and advantageous to the State and the subjects that they should properly understand each other. "Such an arrangement," wrote Runga Charlu, "such an arrangement, by bringing the people in immediate communication with the Government would serve to remove from their minds any misapprehension in regard to the views and actions of the Government and would convince them that the interests of the Government are identical with those of the people."

When the Representative Assembly met

for the first time in 1881 its objects were questioned, its success doubted, its constitution discussed and adversely commented upon, and the whole affair was represented as a well-devised artifice of the fertile brain of the Dewan who saw the necessity of giving some proof of an assumed patriotism to conciliate the indignant Mysoreans whom his towering ambition, his partiality for Madras, and his sudden elevation had offended. But the assembly has survived all such criticisms. During the first two years of the Assembly Runga Charlu carried out only partially the reforms which he intended to institute. He hoped to live long enough to complete them and to see the Mysore province intersected by a number of railway lines. But this was not to be. About the close of 1892 he fell seriously ill. After a wearing illness of some months, he was brought down to Madras for a change but he grew worse and continued to sink until death put an end to his highly useful and honourable career.

Mr. Taylor, his old friend and patron, on hearing of his death wrote that Runga Charlu's " loss will long be felt and mourned by his fellow countrymen, and it will be no easy task to the administration to fill his place." Mr. Powell his old Master said " He was one of my earliest and best pupils and a most honourable and able man. Apart from the loss to his family and his friends, his untimely death is a sad blow to India and Mysore in particular. The advance of a

Hindu to a prominent position amongst statesmen necessarily raises the whole country and is an incentive to his countrymen to persevere in well-doing. So far, it is a consolation that his career has been a most useful and a distinguished one and that his example and his reputation will continue to actuate your countrymen for many years to come. I would urge upon you to have his example before you throughout your lives to aim at being as conscientious and as energetic as he was throughout his lifetime."

Mr. Porter considered Runga Charlu's death an irreparable loss to Mysore. Writing to his son, Mr Porter said: "He had just time to show how much he was able to do when he was taken away. There is nothing I know so full of sadness as a career like that cut short when it was so full of promise. I was wonderfully fond of your father. Of all the men I have met in India, there was no one I was so fond of talking to on all subjects. He was full of ideas and his thoughts were always running on schemes for improving the condition of the people. I can hardly think of that busy brain being still. Then he had a remarkably fine temper and was very pleasant in all his ways. There was not a particle of rancour about him. I feel personally as if there was a great blank in Mysore when he is gone. It is gratifying to hear that he retained his vigour of mind to the last. The *Times* noticed the curious coincidence that the Ministers of Mysore and Hyderabad died within a few days of each other." The late Maharajah of Mysore said that by the death of Runga Charlu he had been deprived of an able, faithful and devoted councillor and that the people of the State had lost a true and sympathetic friend. The Mysoreans who once hated him mustered strong to show their respect for his memory at the meeting held at Bangalore, soon after his death, to concert measures for perpetuating his memory.

A. SESHIA SASTRI, C.S.I.

Amaravati Seshia Sastri was born in the year 1829 in the village of Amaravati situated on the southern bank of the Vettar near Kumbaconum. He was born of poor though respectable parents. Madras was then the only place where any English education was given. Seshia after learning the rudiments of English under two Eurasian teachers, was sent to the Mission School known as Anderson's School in Madras. Here he studied for about two years, when the conversions to Christianity which took place then resulted in the desertion of the school by the students *en masse*. Seshia was next enrolled as a pupil of a school known as Preparatory School, so called because it was preparatory to the establishment of the High School in 1840. Just about that time, the Trustees of Pachaiappa's Charities founded a few scholarships to poor and deserving youths and one of these scholarships was conferred on young Seshia. It was a most timely help to him, for his poor uncle's means were by no means equal to the payment of a school fee of Rs. 4 per mensem. He then obtained a Government scholarship and studied in the High School from 1840 to 1848 under Messrs. White and Bowers in the lower classes and in the higher classes under Messrs. Adam, Gordon and Powell. His career in school was a very distinguished one and in addition to many annual class prizes, he was awarded Pachaiappa's Translation Prize and the first Prize of the Council of Education. He took a first class Proficient's degree in 1848 and left school with the very highest testimonials of character from Messrs Powell and Gordon —the former concluding his certificate with the observation that "he had formed a very high opinion of Seshia's integrity and would not scruple to place the highest confidence in him." The several essays he wrote both in the class room and in open competition for prizes were considered remarkable for one of his age and the speech he delivered on the occasion of laying the foundation-stone of Pachaiappa's Hall in 1846 attracted great attention. The Editor of the *Crescent* spoke of it in terms of great praise and contrasted it with the addresses of one Rajagopal, one of Rev. Anderson's best pupils.

Seshia Sastri entered the Revenue Board as a Clerk on Rs. 25 in September 1848 and was trained under the immediate eye of Sir Henry Pycroft, whose style of drafting official correspondence has become a bye-word in the clerical line of bnsiness. In June 1849, Seshia Sastri accompanied the

Senior Member of the Board, Sir Walter Elliot on his tour through the Northern Circars. Seshia Sastri besides acquiring vast knowledge in clerical work and in all departments of Revenue administration was Sir Walter Elliot's Personal Assistant in the matter of researches botanical, numismatic and antiquarian. Seshia Sastri had special aptitude for such useful work. In May 1851 he became Tahsildar of Masulipatam and in February 1854 was promoted as Naib Sheristadar. In 1855 he was appointed Head Sheristadar at Masulipatam. Here he acquired a thorough knowledge of the Telugu language.

In the Kistna District he displayed his ability in Revenue administration. When he entered Masulipatam it was in a state of demoralization and corruption, but when he left it in 1859 after eight years' active service in that part of the district, it was very nearly a model district. During the year of the Mutiny he displayed great tact and energy in adopting the precautionary measures necessitated by the large Mussulman population at Masulipatam. In 1859, Seshia Sastri was appointed Deputy Collector and made to do duty under Mr. George Noble Taylor, Inam Commissioner. From 1859 to 1866, Seshia Sastri worked in the Inam Commission as Deputy Collector and Special Assistant. During this time, he registered 50,000 original Inam claims and reviewed 2,50,000 letters registered by other Deputy Collectors and controlled a central office of more than 250 clerks. He made a wide research into the various Inam tenures. It was a very laborious and difficult task and was performed with splendid results. In 1866, he was posted as Treasury Deputy Collector. In 1868, he was appointed Head Sheristadar of the Revenue Board which he had left twenty years previously for the Northern Circars.

In July 1872 he was summoned to Travancore as Dewan in succession to Sir Madava Row. The administration of Travancore by Dewan Seshia Sastri extended over a period of five years. The first reform that received his attention was the tabulation of the various kinds of land tenures obtaining in Travancore which was a work of no small difficulty. He then removed some of the abuses largely prevailing in the Government feeding houses. The Salt Department next engaged his attention. The system of measuring out salt by the middlemen who bought it at the first instance from Government and sold it to the people was attended with great fraud. The Dewan ordered the substitution of weight for measure in the sale of salt, a reform which though it could not go direct to the root of the evil was calculated to minimise it. The system of selling salt by weight still afforded opportunites to the seller to cheat the purchaser, but it was hoped that the ignorant multitude could easier detect frauds in weight than in measure. The returns of the Revenue Department were full of entries against defaulters pointing to large and long standing arrears due by them to the State and the Dewan as a relief to the ryots granted large remissions. The voluminous records of all branches of the administration irrespective of the nature and importance of their contents were written on palmyra leaves. Seshia Sastri ordered the substitution of paper for the leaves. In 1875, the Dewan directed his attention to the legal profession in the State which was constituted of men whose knowledge of law was very limited. He insisted upon the members of the Bar undergoing an examination, an ordeal out of which only a small number came unscathed. Those who came out successful were alone declared competent to practise before the highest tribunals of the land and the rest were allowed as a sort of concession to practise in the inferior Courts.

During his administration some important changes were made in the Educational Department. Taluq and Village Schools were multiplied. A class of "attaches" was first formed and attached to the Dewan's office. The posts were given to the most successful pupils who passed out of the College and they were trained to the work in various branches of the administration. After their training was completed, they were absorbed in the several Executive Departments as vacancies arose. The administration of Seshia Sastri in Travancore is best remembered by the cleansing out of the Padmathirtham tank in Travancore and the restoration of the Kochar channel which used in former days to feed the sacred tank perennially and which had been neglected and allowed to fall into disrepair. He is also remembered for the sympathetic way in which he dealt with the large number of immigrants from the neighbouring Districts of Madura and Tinnevelly, whom the famine of 1876-77 drove into Travancore for protection. Many of them were men of means and very respectable, but they could no longer remain in their villages as the deepest wells had run dry and there was absolutely no water for man or beast. It was this dire necessity which compelled them to seek an Asylum in Travancore which had received and protected them on the occasion of a similar dire famine a century before. The refugees, consisted of males, females and children of all ages and ranks. They were welcomed, well-housed, well-fed and altogether well-cared for.

After a service of five years in the Travancore State, Seshia Sastri retired from Travancore on a pension of Rs. 500 in 1877. On the 1st January 1877, he was made a C. S. I. After his retirement, he was engaged in conjunction with Mr. Webster in the distribution of the Mansion House Fund to the sufferers in the great famine of that year, in the Districts of Trichinopoly and Tanjore. He attended the public meeting that was held in Madras for thanking the people of England for their generous help and delivered a speech giving a graphic account of all the measures adopted by His Grace the Duke of Buckingham for the relief of the people. It was just about this time that he was nominated a member of the Madras Legislative Council. Subsequently, he was offered a seat in the Viceregal Legislative Council which he declined.

Meanwhile, the affairs of the small native state of Pudukota had been drifting from bad to worse and the Duke of Buckingham offered the appointment of Dewan of Pudukota to Seshia Sastri in August 1878. At the time he took charge of the administration the coffers of the State were thoroughly empty. The chief source of State revenue was land. The Amani system was then in vogue in the State. This system of collecting revenue was attended with the most disastrous results both to the State and to the ryot. A cumbrous and expensive machinery was maintained at the expense of the State for the purpose of estimating on a field-to-field inspection the produce of the lands with reference to the state of cultivation at the time of the inspection. The ryots were not allowed to reap the crop or store it up unless in the presence of some officials of the State's Agency and as, notwithstanding the large number of officers employed by Government to superintend the reaping of the crops, the presence of these officials could not be secured in every field when the crop was ready for harvest, there was a diminution in the produce owing to the delay in the harvest. This system opened a large door to fraud. The excess of the actual yield over the estimate was never brought into account but divided on the threshing floor in some definite ratio between the ryot and the officer superintending the harvest on behalf of the State. In addition to the loss occasioned to the State by the deliberate reduction of the estimate and by the subsequent fraud of which the State was kept in complete ignorance by the well-concerted action of its interested and corrupt officials, the arrangement of storing up the State's share of the produce was a source of additional loss. The employment of a large number of watchmen from one end of the State to another to guard the paddy on behalf of the State in various places until such time as the price of paddy had sufficiently risen to allow of its being sold with advantage to the State, cost a considerable sum of money which more than counterbalanced the small profit accruing to the State by the rise in the price of paddy. The Dewan, consequently, abolished the Amani system and substituted for it the system of assessment in money. This change considerably enhanced the revenues of the State without in the slightest degree increasing the burden of the ryot.

Simultaneously with the financial improvement in this direction, the Dewan had also been strenuously exerting himself in the direction of reducing the scandalously large palace expenditure. The Dewan spent the surplus thus secured in works of public utility and in making such improvements in the physical condition of the

State as would in a way re-imburse the State of the money expended on them. In 1882, the Rajah's School, was raised to a second Grade College. A Girl's school was also started. The town of Pudukota and its suburbs depended on the adjacent jungles for the supply of fuel and it was clear the jungles would in the course of some years be totally destroyed. The Dewan, therefore, selected suitable sites on the banks of the Palar and directed the planting of thousands of casuarina plants there. The state of the tanks next engaged his attention. The most difficult portion of the programme of rendering the tanks useful as large reservoirs of water was the enormous quantity of slough and silt that had to be removed. Every little village, therefore, within the State was directed to send in all its labourers by rotation and three to seven thousand labourers were every day at work in some tank or other so that the largest of them was cleared of its slough and silt in a very short time. Having dug up the tanks and rendered them useful as reservoirs of water all the year round, the Dewan turned his attention to the improvement of the roads in the capital.

In April 1886 the old Rajah of Pudukotta died leaving behind his grandson, the present Rajah who was a minor. The Dewan was, thereupon, appointed Dewan-Regent. The death of the Rajah armed the Dewan-Regent with greater powers for carrying out some important reforms. The first thing which received his attention after the death of the Rajah was the Appeal Court. He constituted the Pudukotta Chief Court on the 1st January 1887 and modelled it after the Madras High Court. He then took up the question of the enfranchisement of Inams and the resumption of grants of certain description made for services rendered or supposed to be rendered to the State by the holders of the Inams or their ancestors. The first portion of the reform occupied some years, for the Inams had to be measured and their extent ascertained. Any excess found to exist on actual measurement over the extent of the lands originally given by the State was declared the absolute property of the State and the rest was slightly burdened with a small assessment. Other provisions were also made subjecting the Inam lands to increased assessment on the happening of certain contingencies. This reform, no doubt, caused some amount of heart-burning among the Inamdars. But it contributed to a large increase in the State revenue and furnished the Dewan-Regent with funds.

The public buildings in Pudukota form one of the grandest monuments of Seshia Sastri's administration. The various offices of the town were scattered over the whole length and breadth of it and people who had often business to transact in more than one office at about the same time were put to great hardship and inconvenience. The Dewan, therefore, raised a block of buildings to accomodate all the public offices. The construction of works of public utility, the excellent arrangements for lighting the town, the laying and metalling of a number of roads connecting the town with the adjacent districts and important places within the State, the digging of new and the improvement of old tanks, and the impetus given to education generally and female education in particular are some of the salient features of his administration. In one of his administration reports, the Dewan-Regent wrote,—" People who had known the town well ten years ago can hardly recognise it now. New suburbs, new streets, new lanes added to new roads and new tanks and old tanks so improved as not to be easily recognised, all kept in perfect order and cleanliness and all lighted without stint in the dark hours, meet them at every turn and confound them for the nonce." This is indeed a glowing picture but none the less true.

Seshia Sastri retired from the service of Pudukota on the 27th November 1894, the day when the young Tondiman was installed as Rajah. At the installation, Lord Wenlock, Governor of Madras, paid a handsome compliment to him. Addressing the young Rajah, the Governor said :— "The inheritance upon which you are this day entering was twenty years ago financially and in every other respect in a most dilapidated condition. The aspect of affairs is now very different; you will have made over to you a State not only unencumbered with debt but possessing a balance of no less than three lakhs, while there is every prospect of its yielding an increasing revenue if administered with due care. On every side material improvements are visible. Every branch of the administration has been more or less reformed, the revenue has improved, the roads are excellent, and the capital is adorned with modern public buildings. All these are due to the untiring energy and devotion to his duties of Dewan-Regent Seshia Sastri, one of that talented body, the proficients of the High School, so many members of which have taken a prominent and honourable share in public affairs. Seshia Sastri became Dewan in 1878, and after serving your grandfather until his demise in 1886, has since then continued to work for the well-being of the State of Pudukota with great ability and remarkable fidelity and honesty of purpose. The result of his labours has been so successful that what was at the time of his accession to office almost a wreck is at the present moment a prosperous possession. He is now, after a long and trying period of devotion to public service, laying aside official harness in view to enjoying a well-earned repose. I consider that Your Highness owes him a deep debt of gratitude, and I am pleased to learn that you have decided to manifest your appreciation of the service done by him on his retirement in an appropriate manner."

Seshia Sastri has the reputation of being a terse writer. His school essays showed signs of a careful study of English idiom and style. Reports on the history of the Inam Commission which he wrote for Mr. Tom Blair, and his Jamabundi Settlement Reports will amply repay perusal even to this day. His official papers are interesting reading unlike the usual tedious and dull conventional prosaic productions. The late Mr. Justice Holloway complimented him more than once on the excellence of his reports. Seshia Sastri's conversational powers are far above the average. His conversation is easy, flowing and humorous and the apt lines of poetry always ready on his lips make his narrations and descriptions worth listening to. Having experienced the cold touches of poverty in his boyhood, Seshia Sastri deeply sympathises with the poor and he gives to this day unostentatious help to many of his poor relatives and friends. He is now spending his days in honorable retirement on the banks of the Cauvery at Kumbakonam.

ERRATA.

Page 6, line 25, read "is" before the word "still".

„ 31, „ 25, read "1866" for "1886".

„ 131, „ 2, read "1847" for "1837".

„ 145, „ 11, read "numbers" for "members".

„ 146, last line, drop the last word "the".

„ 177, line 9, read "adversely" for "adversedly".